ENDORSEMENTS

"Classical military strategist Carl von Clausewitz wrote of the 'paradoxical trinity' encompassing the collective wills of the government, the military, and the people in order for a Nation to successfully prosecute a war. In the breathtaking book *Betrayed*, we see what happens when one aspect of that that trinity and senior levels of another, through seemingly willful negligence, eschews the trust of the other two. As a former Member of Congress and member of the House Armed Services Committee, I was briefed on the classified details of the mission infamously referred to by call sign *Extortion 17*. Having been a Combat Arms officer in the US Army for 22 years, I was disturbed at several instances where standard TTPs (Tactics, Techniques, and Procedures) were not followed. As well, having been Billy and Karen Vaughn's representative, I know the hurt and anguish of the parents of an elite warrior, their son Aaron, whose life was lost because of a blatant betrayal of the trust they put into their government to protect those who support and defend our Constitution and way of life. *Betrayed* is a must read for those who wish to restore Clausewitz's trinity and ensure that future administrations and military leadership places the safety and well being of our warriors first and foremost."

—Lieutenant Colonel Allen B. West, US Army (Ret.)
Member of 112th Congress

"Billy Vaughn's family story reveals on a smaller scale what has happened to many of our families who have lost loved ones in combat. This book is a must-read for anyone who is getting uneasy about the condition of our military. Billy Vaughn exposes startling revelations as the loss of the brave warriors on board *Extortion 17* expands into larger cover-ups. Questions remain and the surviving families deserve answers—as does the nation!"

—Lieutenant General Tom McInerney, US Air Force (Ret.)

"*Betrayed* is a book that deserves national attention. It is high time it was written. On that terrible day in 2011, hundreds of Americans, family members and friends, including me (a retired SEAL), were directly and grievously affected by the shoot-down of *Extortion 17*. The first thought that ran through my mind was, 'How did the operational commanders of the personnel who died in that helicopter even conceive of such a mission?' That question remains unresolved in my own thinking, and now the possibility of more-nefarious motives has arisen. *Betrayed* examines that possibility in detail, and if it causes an in-depth investigation to be conducted into the entire affair, then Billy Vaughn will have fulfilled his duty to his warrior son, Aaron. Well done, Billy."

—Captain Larry Bailey, (SEAL), US Navy (Ret.)

"When our government and media make our most covert warfighters a public spectacle, putting the operators, their families and the SpecOp Community in clear and present danger, we must ask 'why?', figure out what went wrong, hold people responsible and make sure it does not happen again. Simple.

There are contradictions and suspicions that have surfaced surrounding *Extortion 17* that need investigating. The bodies of American military men (my friends) were damned by an Islamic Imam at an official Ramp Ceremony at the Bagram Airfield, all allowed by US officials. This is pure sacrilege. We the People need to hold our government accountable and the families of the fallen particularly deserve a coherent explanation.

Political correctness, the counter-insurgency strategy and our Rules of Engagement have neutered our warfighter in life or death situations that WE/our government have sent them to do. In a chaotic world on the brink of a religious world war we must, as a people, identify and define our willingness to accept what our warfighters can commit in our defense. This is not an attack on the community or the Navy but a conversation that must be had. Our lives depend on it. It is our civic duty."

—Ben Smith, (Former SEAL), US Navy

"Grief and politics don't mix. When raw, aching grief and the dirtiest kind of politics meet, a hot volcano of pain and outrage erupts that is unstoppable. Like a flame-tipped lance, *Betrayed* takes aim at the lies and secrecy of a government no longer true to the American people -- not even to the families whose sons have paid the ultimate price. What are they hiding? *Betrayed* forces the all-important question forward, past the silence and cover-up, to ensure that we all have the tools we need to get to the truth."

—Diana West, syndicated columnist and author of *American Betrayal: The Secret Assault on Our Nation's Character*

"*Betrayed* is a book that must be read. It is the story of American heroes and how America let them down. While combat losses are sadly inevitable, failure to support our war fighters with every means at our disposal, prioritization of foreign lives over American lives, deference to the enemy ideology of jihad and shariah, and blatant cover-ups about what really happened to the brave men on board *Extortion 17* were not inevitable. We need to know the truth so we can reassert a national policy based on core American principles. *Betrayed* begins that critical process."

–Clare Lopez, Senior Fellow at the Center for Security Policy

BETRAYED

The Shocking True Story of Extortion 17
as told by a Navy SEAL's Father

BILLY VAUGHN

with Monica Morrill & Cari Blake

Patch worn by SEAL Team I during a deployment to Iraq,
designed by Aaron and his teammates

DEDICATION

For Aaron Carson Vaughn,
Special Operations Chief (SEAL)
and more importantly a Father, Husband, Brother,
Son, and my boy.

Billy Vaughn

A portion of all book proceeds will be donated to
Operation 300, a non-profit foundation designed to
create adventure camps for children of the fallen.
For more information, visit

www.operation300.com

BETRAYED:

The Shocking True Story of *Extortion 17* as told by a Navy SEAL's Father

PUBLISHED BY MOLON LABE PUBLISHING, LLC

ISBN: 978-1-62847-683-5

Cover Design by Adam Baldwin; cover image of Navy SEAL Trident by Adam Baldwin from the personal collection of Billy Vaughn. This image is the actual Trident pinned to Aaron's chest upon becoming a Navy SEAL. He presented it to his father on his first trip home after receiving it.

Printed in the United States of America

2013 – First Edition

For more information on Aaron Vaughn, please visit www.forourson.us

Contents

BETRAYED

Introduction

Lieutenant General Jerry Boykin, US Army (Ret.)

As the sun rose over the beaches of Normandy on the morning of June 6, 1944, thousands of young Americans waded through the surf and raced toward the German defenses, intent on bringing WWII to an end and destroying the Nazi regime of Adolf Hitler. Each man on those beaches knew that he had the full support of his nation and of his chain of command. General Dwight Eisenhower, the Allied Commander, had taken a huge risk with an expectation of a huge payoff when he ordered the invasion. He was there to win and he never contemplated anything less.

Although Ike wrote a letter before the invasion accepting responsibility for the failure if the invasion was not successful, he still intended to win the war even if it meant multiple attempts at establishing a beachhead on mainland Europe. Those men who he had ordered into combat would have his full support, and he would trust commanders at all levels to do all they could to defeat the enemy and to protect the lives of their troops. His gamble paid off, the coalition that he lead succeeded, and

Hitler's forces were defeated, restoring sovereignty to the nations of Europe.

For the United States, a new warfare paradigm exists that would make the success of the D-Day efforts doubtful if executed today. In fact, warfare has always been an extension of politics, but after WWII, politics began to impede American war fighting to the extent that victory is fleeting at best and unlikely at worst. Furthermore, the risks to the troops have increased as a result of this shifted paradigm. Commanders are often unable to employ their full capabilities or use their preferred tactics in order to defeat the enemy. The reason is simply that the political considerations have become so dominate that it is nearly impossible to win. Undoubtedly the nature of warfare has changed since WWII, but the imperative to defeat the enemy has not.

"Winning hearts and minds" is a poor substitute for victory over a determined foe. If America does not intend to win, then US Forces should never engage an adversary. "Nation Building" should be done through the NGO and PVO communities and not using trained warriors of the US military. Humanitarian projects are often effective and beneficial in areas where warring factions have disrupted and destroyed the local infrastructure, but the use of the US military for these activities is ill advised due to the overpowering and irresistible political influences. The imperative of providing American Forces with the tools and authority, including the appropriate rules of engagement, to achieve victory and to protect themselves and their coalition partners should always dominate American war fighting. When commanders can no longer make every reasonable effort to ensure the safety of their troops, they should terminate combat operations and withdraw from the battle space. Unfortunately, American commanders in Afghanistan have been forced to deal with an unacceptable choice between meeting the ubiquitous political demands and fighting to win.

The Counter-Insurgency (COIN) strategy that has been pursued by the last two administrations has not succeeded in destroying the Taliban nor in winning the war. Moreover, this strategy has produced the most restrictive Rules of Engagement in modern warfare, jeopardizing the lives of every military member serving in Afghanistan. Commanders have been forced to fight an enemy who knows the US rules well and leverages those restrictions on our warriors to kill and wound our men and women. The days of boldness and audacity by small unit leaders in closing with and destroying an enemy are gone. That type of tactics and strategy has been replaced by a COIN strategy that focuses more on preventing collateral damage at the risk of US lives.

There is no greater example of the results of this approach to warfare than the tragedy of August 6, 2011. It occurred in the Wardak province of Afghanistan, where a US Chinook helicopter, call sign *Extortion 17*, was shot down in a Taliban ambush, killing thirty Americans and seven Afghan National Army (ANA) personnel and one interpreter. Fifteen of those killed were some of America's finest and most dedicated warriors from Seal Team Six, the same unit that killed Usama Bin Laden. One of the SEALS on *Extortion 17* was Aaron Vaughn, the son of Karen and Billy Vaughn.

While seeking the details of the shoot down that took Aaron's life, Billy and Karen uncovered some startling facts about the mission that *Extortion 17* was on the night that their son died in a fiery crash west of Kabul, Afghanistan. After receiving a heavily redacted copy of the after action report of the incident, Aaron's parents began to have serious questions about the events surrounding that Special Operation. Simply wanting to know the facts about Aaron's death, the Vaughns asked some hard questions of the chain of command. They were shocked to discover that no effort was made to eliminate known threats around the landing zone (LZ) before the Chinook landed even though there were multiple opportunities and means to do so.

The Vaughns were also surprised to discover that the Chinook that Aaron and his mates were on was not a Special Operations helicopter with the most modern technology. Rather it was a nearly fifty-year-old aircraft with minimal capabilities flown by courageous pilots with no experience with Special Operations. The US Special Operations Command (USSOCOM) in Tampa has spent untold millions of dollars equipping their SOF helos with the finest technology available; why were these SEALS not on one of these? The Vaughns simply wanted to know why. Was it because there were none available or were there higher priorities than this mission? These are not unreasonable questions from a grieving family.

They were also startled to find that seven of the ANA soldiers who died in the crash were not even manifested for the flight. In fact, they were substituted at the last minute for seven other ANA personnel who actually had been manifested. The conclusion that they came to was that neither they nor the other families were being provided with the whole story about the operation that took the lives of their sons, husbands, and brothers.

Overhearing a senior commander tell another family of one of the dead SEALS that the primary focus in Afghanistan was to "win the hearts and minds," the Vaughns were enraged. The idea that the sensitivities and feelings of the Afghani people was more important than the lives of America's warriors was more than they could tolerate. Was that the message or did they simply not understand the words and meaning of the

4

senior officer? They decided that they must act and call for accountability and truth.

In their minds and that of other families, there were simply too many contradictions and half-truths for them to accept the story that they had been given regarding the events of August 6, 2011, and they would not rest until they had been provided accurate details. Was there some kind of cover up? Were their sons targeted deliberately because of their team's involvement in the Bin Laden operation? Who were the seven ANA soldiers that were added at the last minute? Why was a Non-Special Operations helo used? These and myriad other questions have yet to be answered but must be before the Vaughns and other families will cease in their efforts to get to the facts of the deaths of their sons. This book is part of their painful quest for a full accounting. It is a fascinating story of incredible courage and sacrifice, government deceit, and the changing nature of warfare.

BETRAYED

Prologue

Billy Vaughn - A Father's Perspective

*"People sleep peaceably in their beds at night only because
rough men stand ready to do violence on their behalf."
– Attributed to George Orwell*

When your son dedicates his life to defending and protecting his country—our country—the feeling of pride in his decisions, mixed with concern over what those decisions could cost him, is overwhelming. In the back of your mind, you always know there's a faint possibility that one day he might not make it back, but that is not a thought you allow yourself to dwell on.

I am immensely proud of my son, Aaron Vaughn, a member of the most elite assault force in the world, the Navy SEALs. He fought with honor, and with more courage and skill than most American citizens could conceive of, even when facing their greatest challenges. That's what he was trained to do; what he lived to do.

Aaron lost his life over seven thousand miles from home, fighting in Afghanistan, for the republic he loved. The record will show the Taliban made the shot that took down *Extortion 17*, but our government's refusal to recognize the enemy and its ideology may have shouldered even greater responsibility.

What follows in this book are the facts of the events that transpired before, during, and after that fateful day, August 6, 2011, when a chopper with the call sign *Extortion 17* was shot down. That mission resulted in the largest loss of life in Navy SEAL history. It was the last day of my son's life.

It was the first day of the rest of mine.

The operation began on August 5, 2011, at about 8:30am EST, as a group of fearless, rough men—most of them Navy SEALs, the best of the best America has to offer—were getting ready for their night shift in the Tangi River Valley, Wardak Province, Afghanistan. Those men set out as they did on every operation with the desire, duty, and obligation to confront a violent enemy, an enemy who was set on the destruction of all the SEALs loved and had left behind. These great American heroes climbed on their antiquated ride to work, a CH-47D helicopter normally used for transporting cargo. Just before they were dropped at their destination, they were shot out of the sky and fell to their deaths. It is quite possible my son and the twenty-nine other American warriors aboard *Extortion 17* lost their lives because their leaders decided political posturing and ill-gotten gain was more important than bringing them home.

During the many months since that day, I have scoured documentation, spoken with other bereaved families, conducted interviews with military insiders, asked for help from the media, and met with members of Congress. As I have navigated through the moments leading up to the shoot-down that took my son's life and the lives of twenty-nine other brave Americans in one devastating instant, I've discovered the downing of *Extortion 17* was not what it appeared to be. It was a reckless loss of life.

Is my son dead because policy and strategy made our Special Operation Forces vulnerable? The loss of *Extortion 17* is not an isolated incident; it is a continuum of errant government policies and procedures. Our government would rather coddle the enemy in blatant appeasement than use our total force capability to neutralize them. Our government would rather "win hearts and minds" than properly vet the Afghanis who fight alongside our men and women in theater. Our government prefers to give the enemy the benefit of the doubt rather than ultimately keeping our homes and families safe here on American soil.

Let me be clear, in no way is my hunt for the truth meant as a slam on the military rank and file. No one appreciates these service men and women more than I do—my boy was a SEAL! But I do know mistakes were made and cover-ups have occurred. This book is an endeavor to expose denials and get answers from the National Security team, whose strategy has become weak-minded and political, and as a result, is now failing our great military.

In her testimony before Congress, when being questioned on what led up to the deaths in Benghazi, Libya, of four brave Americans, Secretary of State Hillary Clinton asked, "What difference, at this point, does it make?"

In return, let me ask her this: What difference, at this point, Mrs. Clinton, does it make that on September 11, 2001, forty Americans on board Flight 93 gave their lives to save our Capitol building and their fellow citizens? What difference, at this point, does it make that in the 1950s, tens of thousands of Americans went overseas to hold back the tide of Communism that was determined to spread tyranny across the world? In World Wars I and II, what difference does it make, at this point, to our allies in the Americas, Europe and Asia that millions of Americans fought around the world for the freedom of mankind? During the Civil War, what difference, at this point, does it make that massive amounts of blood were shed on the battlefields of our own soil to achieve true freedom for Americans of every creed and color? And finally, what difference at this point, Mrs. Clinton, does it make that General George Washington led a grossly ill-prepared, ill-equipped, rag-tag group of volunteers in the middle of the night on December 25, 1776, across the Delaware River in Trenton, New Jersey, and surprised a sleeping Hessian army to win a battle that would turn the tide in the fight for our nation's freedom?

As the father of a fallen hero, Mrs. Clinton, this entire book is dedicated to answering your insulting question. Because when Americans heed the call and agree to risk their lives in the name of freedom, it is the understanding of who the enemy is, what their capabilities are, and what the fight is about that makes the difference. In our current war on terrorism—a war imposed on us—if our nation's leaders don't understand and are not willing to admit the Islamic Jihadist enemy we now face means to take us over and kill us, then there is no point in another American sacrificing his or her life before our ultimate doom.

In the case of Benghazi, Mrs. Clinton, according to your testimony, it was beneath you to know what was happening there before disaster struck. Therefore, nothing was done to either prevent or intervene in that horrible loss of life. Just the same, in the case of *Extortion 17*, the lives of our once elusive, but now very exposed elite warriors depended on our nation's leaders not living in such carelessness and denial. Those Navy SEALs and their fellow service members' lives depended on the intricately built cover that once shrouded them in mystery, enabling them to be the "tip of the spear" no one saw coming. That cover is now gone—it makes a difference.

I don't want to write this book. As a father, reliving this is not a road I would ever choose to travel. But I *have* to write this book because we deserve to know the truth, the American people deserve answers and our government, steeped in denial, needs a wakeup call.

Aaron receiving his BUD/S graduation certificate.

1

A Fallen Angel Over Afghanistan

*Then I heard the voice of the Lord saying,
"Whom shall I send? And who will go for
us?" And I said, "Here am I. Send me!"*

- Isaiah 6:8 NIV

AH-64 Pilot 2: "I just saw a flash. Did you see a flash?"

AH-64 Pilot 1: "Yeah, they're being shot at."

AH-64 Pilot 2: "What is that?"

AH-64 Pilot 1: "Dude, I think they just got shot."

AH-64 Pilot 2: "Extortion 17 – are you shot?"

AH-64 Pilot 1: "Are you on that?"

AH-64 Pilot 2: "I'm on it, sir? Extortion 17 is down. I repeat, Extortion 17 is down."

AH-64 Pilot 2: "Coalition traffic; we have a Fallen Angel. Fallen Angel. It's Extortion 17. (expletive)"

AH-64 Pilot 1: "Roger. We have a Fallen Angel. Extortion 17 was shot down in the Tangi River Valley. (expletive)"

AH-64 Pilot 2: "1 this is 2. Do you have anything? We've got nothing at this time. We've got a wreckage on fire."

AH-64 Pilot 1: "Do you see any survivors down there?"

AH-64 Pilot 2: "I'm not seeing any. No, I'm not seeing anything right now. It's a ball of fire. It looks bad." … "All right. Oh, God. (Expletive). Man. I'm not seeing anybody, any survivors." [1]

It was August 5, 2011, around mid-day, at the Wardak Province, Afghanistan, Forward Operating Base (FOB). A high-value Taliban target, Qari Tahir, had been located in a small village in the southern region of the Tangi River Valley. After a few hours of planning, it was decided to deploy Army Rangers as a strike force to capture Tahir. At that point, two teams loaded up antiquated CH-47D Chinook choppers with call signs of *Extortion 16* and *Extortion 17*. The choppers were escorted to their infiltration position south of the targeted village by two AH-64D Apaches. Upon Ranger insertion, the Apaches joined an AC-130 Spectre Gunship and other Intelligence Surveillance and Reconnaissance (ISR) already underway. The two CH-47Ds returned to the FOB to await their exfiltration orders.

As the Rangers advanced, the Air Weapons Team circling above noticed two men fleeing the rear, eastern quarter of the targeted village. These squirters (escapees) were moving northward along the edge of the valley, successfully evading their would-be captors. Members of SEAL Team VI watched intently via surveillance capabilities, standing ready to assist if needed. They believed one of those squirters was Qari Tahir, himself, since that type of evasion is the typical modus operandi for the Taliban's protection of their true target.

At approximately 2:20 a.m., after fastidious observation of the target's strategic movement and with a coalition of forces from both sides of the valley, the order came down to initiate a Quick Reactionary Force (QRF) and move in for the capture. It was then that thirty fearless American warriors, along with eight Afghanis, boarded *Extortion 17* and headed out for their night's work. The on-board team included:

7 Unidentified Afghan commandos

1 Afghan interpreter

5 US Army and US Army National Guard flight crew members

3 US Air Force members of the 24th Special Tactics Squadron

22 US Navy personnel, including:

5 US Navy SEAL Team support members and one working dog

17 US Navy SEALs—part of the most elite assault force the world has ever known.

After a short flight, the landing zone was in sight. But on that fateful night, *Extortion 17* would never touch down. According to the Report of Investigation, from the dark of night, three rocket-propelled grenades (RPGs) were fired in rapid succession. The first RPG flew below the Chinook, but the second made contact in what the military would later describe as a "one-in-a-million shot." It struck a rotor blade on the aft (rear) pylon, shearing off ten and a half feet of the blade. The third shot flew above the falling chopper.

Within a matter of seconds, while spinning violently out of control, the aft, then forward pylons both separated from the aircraft. The main fuselage dropped vertically into a dry creek bed, immediately engulfed in a large fireball, causing multiple secondary explosions of fuel and munitions until the aircraft burned out several hours later.

There were no survivors.

These thirty brave Americans were more than just warriors. They were husbands, fathers, brothers, and sons.

My son, Aaron Carson Vaughn, was one of them.

After my boy died, we were given documents from the Navy that described the incident as I have shared it here. Among those documents is the transcript between the Apache Helicopter pilots, AH-64 Pilot 1 and AH-64 Pilot 2 as they witnessed the firing upon and subsequent explosion of *Extortion 17*. I began this chapter with the last words spoken in the last seconds of my son's life.

Since the day I read that transcript, I cannot help but replay that conversation over and over in my mind. I do not think a day goes by when those words do not resonate back to me. Aaron was a member of US Navy SEAL Team VI. He was one of America's proud, elite warriors.

I miss him.

Aaron was our firstborn and only son, delivered to us in Union City, Tennessee, on June 24, 1981. He was such a blessing from the Lord. Aaron brought so much happiness for my wife, Karen, and me. As the first grandchild on both sides of our families, he was greatly loved and adored.

Aaron was a passionate young boy with a determined spirit. As he grew, I would often describe him as tender, yet equally fearless. He could be tough as nails and, still, he was completely heart-broken when his younger sister told him the truth about Santa Claus and the Tooth Fairy. But the strongest impression Aaron left on all who knew him was his determination for good to triumph. He had discernment uncharacteristic for a young boy, and he carried it into adulthood. Aaron was naturally drawn to the history of brave men who fought for what they knew was right. He was never afraid to recognize or call out evil.

Back in those days, I worked a graveyard shift to support my family and so nightly it was left to Karen to be with the children. One night, at age five, Aaron asked his mom if they could talk for a few minutes as she tucked him into bed. Aaron told her that he, "just had to ask Jesus into his heart."

Karen and I brought our children to church regularly so it was natural for Aaron to be drawn to God, but Karen questioned him to be sure he knew what he was saying. Aaron convinced her that he understood the purpose of salvation and confessed to his mom, "Jesus did it for me. He died for me so I could go to heaven."

That night, our young boy prayed the "sinner's prayer" and committed his life to Christ. Even though he was only five, we never doubted the sincerity of the decision he made.

By the time Aaron was eight years old, his fearlessness had kicked into full gear. On our farm in West Tennessee, we were installing fence posts around the property one day when Aaron said, "Daddy, I want to be a Ranger when I grow up because they are the roughest fighting force in the military."

I was a bit stunned by what he said, but not completely surprised because, even as a boy, he always chose the tougher path. I told him the Rangers were among the most elite fighting force, yet I explained to Aaron that the SEALs also held that honor, even a notch above. I clarified that SEALs stood for and covered vast geography: Sea, Air and Land. He thought about it briefly and then changed his mind. He was going to be a Navy SEAL.

At the time, he had no idea the detours he would take before finally becoming one. Nor could I have imagined the huge challenges he would face to achieve that dream.

Growing up on a farm, Aaron preferred hunting over cartoons, darts over hopscotch, tackle instead of flag football, dodge ball over tag, and BB gun fights to bowling. He loved God, his family, and his country. Aaron never took for granted that he had been blessed enough to have been born in the United States of America, the land of the free and the brave. That awareness always seemed to shape Aaron's ideals and his plans for the future.

When Aaron was in junior high he earned a spot on the football team. He played defensive end, gaining a starting position on his high school team by his sophomore year. In 1998, our family moved from Tennessee to Southeast Florida, and Aaron began playing football at his new high school.

During practice, the day before the season opener of his senior year, Aaron suffered a terrible injury and blew out his left knee. His ACL was obliterated. He ended up in surgery where they replaced it. Once Aaron was back on his feet, he worked hard in rehabilitation. But eight months after his surgery, he took on a pick-up game of basketball after school one day and blew his left knee out again. This time, the doctors could not offer any hope. The surgeon told us there was simply nothing left to work with. Aaron knew at that point his athletic career and his dreams of becoming a SEAL were over.

He was devastated. There were lots of tears and lots of questions. But rather than giving up, he quietly put his mind and body into his physical therapy.

By 2000, Aaron's focus and life had changed direction. He enrolled in Indian River Community College (now State College) and received an associate's degree in golf course management. The Jupiter Island Club Golf Course, one of the most exclusive golf courses in the United States, had generously given him a full scholarship. Employed full-time with a bright future, he was on a new path to success and everything seemed to be smooth sailing. My son worked in a picturesque setting, surrounded by his passion of sports, with a new sense of contentment. Until the unthinkable happened

—September 11, 2001.

Looking back, I have to ask myself if the terrorist attacks of that day truly were "unthinkable" events. Osama bin Laden was a self-proclaimed enemy of America during the Clinton Administration and a known threat at that time. For years, the Clinton Administration had refused to heed warnings, to take action when other governments offered the instigating enemy up to us, or take Osama bin Laden out when we had the chance.[2]

This lack of will ultimately changed the path of Aaron's life, our family, and countless other American families.

After that fateful day, Aaron knew he had no other alternative. The path of the plush green island with palm trees was not going to be his future. Despite all the obstacles that had jumped in his way before, he had to renew his dreams and fulfill his destiny to become a Navy SEAL.

He became even more engrossed in the efforts to rehab his knee, but kept his transformed determination a secret from everyone. What held everything together for my six-foot-four-inch son's left knee was his continual musculature strengthening and his faith in God's plan for him. Aaron worked his leg diligently with that unwavering "Aaron" reputation, his "never-quit" spirit.

For more than nine months, he never said a word to us about what he was planning. In June 2002, on his twenty-first birthday, he announced that he had enlisted in the Navy. He confessed to us that on his application he had lied about not having any past injuries.

I did not know what to say. After his injury, I never considered the possibility he could still become a Navy SEAL. I had no negative feelings about his decision. I wanted to be as supportive as possible, but I also wanted to be realistic. I told him, "Son, I'm so proud of your desire, but you do realize that if you do not make it as a SEAL, you're going to be stuck on a boat, right?" I told him this as a bit of a warning because I knew Aaron did not want to be on a ship—he wanted to be engaged directly with the enemy.

But as it turned out, Aaron did not need my concerns. He flew through all his physical, psychological, and mental tests with great success. Aaron started basic training in November 2002, finally realizing the dream of his childhood. This was the beginning of a long process. Karen and I were totally supportive and prayed for Aaron continuously, knowing that whether or not he would actually make it would ultimately be up to God. With each phase of training more difficult than the last, he excelled beyond expectation. But making it through BUD/S (Basic Underwater Demolition/SEAL) was only the beginning. It took three years of this intense training before Aaron actually deployed as a Navy SEAL.

When Aaron's dreams eventually came true, he jumped in with both feet and loved serving his country. As he deployed for the first time, I wrote him this letter that his wife later returned to me from among his personal effects:

Son,

Let me start by saying I am proud of you beyond expression. In my mind and heart you are a great

American. America symbolizes the very best in human or earthly terms of what mankind should be. Son, you have become a man among men, one who has accomplished what most never will. I never thought years ago that you would do this. Not that I didn't think you could, but that you never had to, for me to be proud of you. Now I am both proud and thankful "beyond measure" for you. People like you do what you do so that people like us can live like we live. Even though you have accomplished much, you will also always be my boy. I love you, Aaron, more than life itself. I look forward to the day when you feel your mission is accomplished and you can be with us in [a] normal setting. I miss you much when you're away. Today will be one of the hardest days in the life of your mom and me. Proud of you, and for you, but at the same time so fearful of the days and months to come. There is comfort in knowing you will be working with men like you who have courage and are willing to do for you what I know you would do for them. The greatest comfort however will come from knowing you're in the hands of our great and merciful God, and know that you love Him. Since you have been a baby, His mighty hand has covered you, not mine, and I thank Him for that. Aaron, I pray you will trust Him and seek Him day by day, hour by hour, and minute by minute. Aaron, you have accomplished much, but you are about to enter your greatest challenge and you <u>must</u> rely on God more than you ever have. I pray for courage for you. I pray you'll always be honorable. I pray God will give discernment in all situations. I pray, son, He will give you everything you need to do what great soldiers have to do. Son, you are great in my eyes and you have earned my utmost respect. You will, most of all, always be my son. Please do what you can to come home safely. What an honor to be called Dad by you.

Love,
Dad

Aaron was an "all or nothing" man, the kind of man who did everything in the most extreme way. I knew he would make a great Navy SEAL. But it was hard for his mother and me. We realized early on we had to place him in God's hands.

After serving in SEAL Team I for several years, he met a beautiful Washington Redskins cheerleader whose squad was overseas entertaining the troops with the USO. They soon fell in love and planned to marry. When he was on leave, they moved all of his things to the East Coast before the wedding so they could start their life together. By that time, Aaron had begun selection and training with the Naval Special Warfare Development Group and was hoping to move up to his ultimate goal of joining Team VI.

The day before the wedding, I was sitting with him in the car. We were waiting for the ladies to come out of a store when he received a call from Command at Coronado. I could tell he wasn't happy with the news he received. Once he got off the phone, he explained that there had been too many issues with training incidents and accidents, and they needed to bump up the number of instructors. Naval Special Warfare (NSW) wanted him for the job.

As I began to give him advice, "Son, you know..."

Aaron interrupted me. "I know, Dad, if this is happening it's God's will, and it's for a good reason."

After the wedding, it would be two years before they would release him to move up. Looking back, it certainly was God's blessing in disguise. The delay gave Aaron and Kimberly the chance to establish their marriage and start a family. They never regretted having that extra time together.

With his career back on track, he endured several months of the most rigorous training offered in the military. Upon successful completion of this training in December of 2010, he reported to his assigned duty—now a proud member of SEAL Team VI. At this point in his career, Aaron had completed numerous operations around the world, including several combat deployments to Afghanistan and Iraq.

By the time of the *Extortion 17* shoot-down in 2011, Aaron had a loving wife, two adorable small children, parents and sisters who had almost as much pride as they had love for him, and two precious young nieces. Before his final deployment, we had just celebrated his thirtieth birthday. Our family was happy, blessed, and growing.

Aaron was a highly decorated combat veteran with numerous awards including the Joint Service Achievement Medal with Valor, Navy and Marine Corps Achievement Medal with Valor, Combat Action Ribbon, Good Conduct Medal, Iraq Campaign Medal, Afghanistan Campaign Medal, Global War on Terrorism (Service) Medal, Global War on Terrorism (Expeditionary) Medal, the Defense Meritorious Service Medal, and numerous other personal and unit decorations. He was posthumously awarded the Purple Heart and the Bronze Star Medal with Valor.

His commander at the US Naval Special Warfare Development Group (DEVGRU) told me Aaron was a "fearless leader, headed to the top." I was told by many of his peers that Aaron was one of the most effective operators they had ever been around and that he was a "light for

Christ in a dark world." His chaplain told Karen and me, "If you gave me five men like Aaron, I could conquer the world."

It was powerful to hear others describe your son as the man you always thought him to be.

2

Sunrise
"The Dawn of the Rest of My Life"

Greater love hath no man than this; that a man lay down his life for his friend.

- John 15:13 KJV

August 6, 2011 fell on a Saturday. Early that morning around three o'clock, I woke up in Burlington, Washington (north of Seattle). I began my day with a prayer and asked the Lord's protection over my family. At the end of my prayer, I repeated that request and I remember saying, "especially for Aaron, whatever he is doing today."

That day, my family was spread out across the globe. Aaron was on deployment in Afghanistan. His wife Kimberly, who had recently given birth to their second child, was in Virginia with her parents. My wife was at home in Florida, as were my daughters, my son-in-law, and my other grandchildren. I was on the opposite corner of the country on my way to deliver a camper trailer to Vancouver Island, British Columbia.

It was a pitch-black morning, hours before the sunrise. I was on the West Coast surrounded by nothing but land on Interstate 5. As I always did while on the road in the mornings, I tuned in to Fox News on satellite radio. But on *this* morning, I caught a quick report that "thirty-one" American soldiers had been killed in a helicopter crash in Afghanistan. My heart stopped for a second. I said silently, "Lord, I pray that Aaron wasn't on that chopper."

But, just as that thought entered my mind, I felt like a dog. What right did I have to even think such a thing? Thirty-one other families had lost someone they loved. Of course, I never wanted Aaron hurt, but I realized that if *my* son was not involved in the crash, someone else's son was.

Moments later, the story came across the radio with additional details. This time, the report was more specific. The reporter used the words, "Special Forces."

Finally, a third report came. I heard the words, "Special Forces with Afghan Commandos in the Wardak Province," and it hit far too close to home. Each update painted a more vivid picture. Special Forces. Wardak Province. Working with Afghan Commandos.

That was Aaron's team...

Although I had put it off as long as I could, I finally called Karen. It was around 7:30am EST when I told her what I had heard. We agreed she would try to get hold of Aaron's friends, but she was unsuccessful. Next, we decided to alert Kimberly's parents that there was some reason for concern. We worried that Kimberly might turn on the TV and learn about the chopper crash that way. Of course, we still didn't know if Aaron was involved, but we didn't want unnecessary anxiety to be created for Kimberly. We wanted things to be as calm as possible for her and our grandchildren while we gathered the facts.

After hanging up with Karen, I called our oldest daughter Tara and informed her of the crash. I told her there was probably nothing to it, but asked her to please go and be with her mom. I didn't want Karen to be alone. Tara began to cry. Aaron was her big brother, and they had grown up with an extraordinary closeness.

Our teenage daughter, Ana, was spending the night with a friend. In those early moments, I decided against calling her since I wanted to protect her from needless worry. She was our baby, and I felt the need to shield her.

Next, I called my brother and told him the report. "Are they saying there are SEALs on board?" he asked with concern.

"No."

"Well maybe none of them were SEALs."

"If there were thirty Special Operators on board," I said, "Chances are, some of them were SEALs."

After that call, I was engaged in a brief conversation with two Canadian fishermen, but my mind and heart were on an event that had occurred some 7,000 miles away. While we were standing on the loading ramp to the ferry to Vancouver Island, our discussion was interrupted by a call back from my daughter. She was crying.

What I heard next were three words for which I could never have prepared myself: "Daddy, he's dead." Tara is married and has a family of her own. She hadn't called me "Daddy" in years.

The words cut to the depth of my heart. I didn't have a response. Just, "Okay, Baby, I'll call you right back."

That call had come way too quickly, for with those words, it was final.

Hope for my son's life was lost.

Later on, I learned that Karen had called Kimberly's parents' home, and they agreed to try and help get confirmation, one way or another. Soon after that, Karen called their house again to give an update.

Kimberly's father answered the phone. "Karen, it's bad."

Karen responded, "Yeah, I know it's bad, I've seen some information about the crash on Facebook."

Kimberly's father interrupted her, nearly unable to speak. "You don't understand. The Navy is here...Aaron was on the helicopter and there were no survivors."

Before the Navy arrived, Kimberly had been warned by her mother that the announcement of a helicopter crash had been on the news. Hearing about the shoot-down, she immediately checked Skype on her computer and saw that Aaron was connected. Relieved, she picked up her daughter, and proceeded upstairs to join her parents for breakfast. As she reached the landing, she heard the doorbell ring and saw her father open the front door. What she saw made her collapse on the floor. There, making their way into the foyer from the long walkway up to the house, were men in Navy uniforms.

As soon as I hung up the phone with my daughter, I climbed into my truck to drive it up the ramp. Almost instantly, my sister Kelly called.

"Are you all right?"

"Yeah, I'm all right," I said, while managing the steering wheel to load the truck on the ferry.

"Are you sure?" Kelly was full of doubt.

"What do you know?" I asked.

"Well, Karen called and asked us to pray that Aaron wouldn't be on the chopper."

"Aaron was on the chopper." The words felt surreal. "He's gone, Kelly."

"Oh no, Billy! Oh no!" I had never heard my sister cry with such desperation before. She agreed to drive to our parents' home to be with them after I called with the news.

I called my parents' home just as they were getting out of bed. My dad answered from the living room, and I immediately told him, "There has been a helicopter crash in Afghanistan."

Dad responded, "They are talking about it right now on the TV."

At that moment my mom picked up the phone in their bedroom. I could still hear the television in the background. My dad was watching Fox News. I thought my father handed over the phone to my mom, and I assumed I was just talking to her when I said, "Aaron is gone."

Mom fell over on their bed from the shock. Dad was still on the line in the living room. I heard him cry out, "Oh no, no!"

When my mom managed to speak again a short while later, she asked, "Oh no, Son, what happened?"

"A helicopter was shot down and he was in it."

"Oh Son, where are you?"

"I'm on a ferry," I replied.

"Does Karen know? Who is with her?"

"Tara." I said. "Mom—I prayed for him this morning and he was already gone." My mind flooded with chaos and confusion.

Then my mom said, with her soft, reassuring voice, "Son, I'm so sorry you are so far away and I can't comfort you, and I'm so sorry that Karen is in Florida." Then she gave me the best advice a mother could give her son. "All we can do right now is stand on our faith because that's all we have."

Deep down, although we all knew it could happen, we were unprepared for this shocking news.

After all of the phone calls were over, I took a deep breath. Karen was there with the rest of our family in Florida, and friends had begun to gather at our house to pray and lend their support; Aaron's young family was with his in-laws; my sister was there to care for and comfort our parents. All my loved ones were being comforted amidst this tragic news—*that* was what mattered. Now it was time for me to make my way home.

By this time, I had already parked my Dodge. It had been a dark morning. Just as I set foot on the deck, a glow of light began to flood the sky as the sun rose. After all the phone calls and engine noise, now all I could hear were the waves embracing the ship's hull as I slowly made my way to Vancouver Island. I stood at the top deck of the ferry, facing northwest, looking out at the Strait of Georgia between Vancouver Island and the mainland. The light intensified as it reflected on the ocean's surface, and in all of my deliberately suppressed emotions, I was now overwhelmed by the stunning image of nature confronting me. I watched the incredible sunrise, the red of dawn, and felt as though it was just God, Aaron, and me.

Finally, I said, "It's a beautiful morning, isn't it, son?"

It may sound strange, but after Tara confirmed that Aaron was dead, in the midst of the deepest pain I had ever experienced, I found a little comfort in knowing the Lord was not shocked by this news. He knew this day would come. Our great God had *always* known that this day would come, all the way back to when Aaron was an eight-year-old boy and first decided what he wanted to do with his life.

It was then I realized how thankful I was that God doesn't let us know about these things ahead of time. The Lord also knew that my entire family would need Him at this moment. He began to provide me with both friends and strangers to help me through those first hours until I could get home to my family.

At some point I received a phone call from Chuck, who had been our Pastor in Tennessee from 1986 until 1992. He and his wife Sara had been close family friends throughout those years. The two of them were at a conference when Sara noticed a comment on Facebook: "Pray for the Vaughn Family."

About an hour after they read the Facebook message, Chuck called me, "Billy, I've heard about the helicopter crash. Is it true...?"

I interrupted him, "Yes Chuck, it's true." I then told him I was on a ferry in Canada of all places.

We spoke about Aaron further, and then Chuck prayed with me. He stayed on the line for about thirty minutes. Chuck was our pastor when Aaron was five years old and had accepted Jesus into his heart, and he was our pastor when Aaron was baptized. That call from Chuck was a gift of compassion, and was so well timed. The love and concern extended to us through long-standing friends who knew Aaron as a young boy had a depth of meaning to me beyond expression.

Karen and I talked over the phone several times thereafter, but we weren't capable of speaking about the details of our only son that day. I remember her saying, "I'm so sorry, honey. I'm so sorry you've lost your son," several times. Most of our discussions concerned how I was going to get back to Florida from the other side of the continent.

Amidst such dreaded news, I noticed Karen had an unexpected calm in her voice. She was resting in the Lord, and it was uplifting to hear this when she spoke so soothingly. I loved my wife, but it was moments like this that strengthened my devotion to her. Even in the midst of our greatest pain, our faith in Jesus made this situation well with our souls.

Through the extended kindness of strangers on the ferry and even my clients, I managed to immediately drop off the trailer and return on the same ferry and catch one of the last flights out of Seattle.

To this day, I don't know the names of everyone who rushed to Karen to lend their support, but I was glad to know our house was filled with a multitude of friends. Friends like Al, who told me to drive my truck to the Seattle airport because he and his wife had already purchased my ticket back home. Jim, who jumped on a plane to Seattle so he could drive my truck back to Florida. Sal and Anita, who had been vacationing on the west coast of Florida, but dropped everything to head back immediately upon receiving the news. And Hoss, who called to tell me he'd lowered our flag to half-staff.

Two couples: Hoss and Linda, and Norm and Casi, had known Aaron longer than any of our friends in Florida. They became a part of his life in 1998, when we first moved there, and it was good to know these two families were with Karen and my daughters as I was making my way home.

Much later that day, I was finally in the airport sitting at the gate, when out of nowhere I heard my mother's voice. I thought for an instant I must have been imagining things. Then my eyes became riveted on the TV monitor.

There, for all to see, was a picture of my boy's face.

It slowly dawned on me that somehow the reporters at CNN had already tracked down my mother in Tennessee. They had her on the phone and were showing Aaron's picture on the screen as mom relayed the details of the last conversation she had with her beloved grandson. I did not recognize the CNN correspondent, but this is how he proceeded with the interview:[1]

CNN: We know those killed in action were heroes choosing to fight for their country. But now, we're learning the details that hint of the devastation their families are feeling, and we know one of the SEALs,

Aaron Carson Vaughn, was the father of a two-year-old and a two-month-old baby. Geneva Carson Vaughn is his grandmother. She joins me now on the phone from Union City, Tennessee. First Mrs. Vaughn, we are deeply sorry for your loss and please convey that to your family. How did you learn that Aaron had been killed?

Mrs. Vaughn: His father, my son, called me after he found out, about eight o'clock this morning.

CNN: Did military officials tell you or your son anything about the attack and if the Taliban were responsible, did they even go into that?

Mrs. Vaughn: No. All I know about that is what I saw on the news. That the Taliban said that they shot the helicopter down that my grandson was in.

CNN: Can you tell us about Aaron? He lived in Virginia Beach, right?

Mrs. Vaughn: Yes, he was stationed in Virginia Beach with his wife and two children.

CNN: And he had a two-year-old?

Mrs. Vaughn: A two-year-old little boy, he'll be two in September, and a two-month-old baby girl. Aaron only got to see her for two weeks. He was deployed when she was two weeks old.

CNN: And his wife? How is she doing?

Mrs. Vaughn: His wife, Kimberly. Kimberly right now is with her parents in [redacted], Virginia, with the children. She went there to stay until Aaron came home from his deployment.

CNN: We're looking at a picture of him on television now, and the last time you saw him and spoke to him, you had a very nice conversation with him. Can you tell us about it?

Mrs. Vaughn: Yes. Yes, I did. It was Aaron's birthday in June, he turned 30, and I told him to be careful. And he said, "Granny, don't worry about me." He said, "I'm not afraid because I know where I'm going if something happens to me." Aaron was a Christian and he stood firm in his faith.

CNN: And you said you know he's with the Lord now.

Mrs. Vaughn: He's with the Lord now, and I'll see him again someday—and that's what the family is standing on now, is faith. We know that God is in control, and we know that He took Aaron for a reason, we don't know what, but we know that He took Aaron for a reason, and the rest of 'em too.

CNN: Aaron knew the dangers and the last time you spoke to him, he said, "Grandma, don't worry about me."

Mrs. Vaughn: That's what he said.

CNN: Why'd he say that to you?

Mrs. Vaughn: As a brave warrior, Aaron was brave, but yet, he was a gentle man. He loved his family, he loved his country, and he was willing to give his life to protect his family and protect his country. He was a great American.

CNN: Listen, Aaron and many like him go off to war and fight these wars for the American people, and they are the reason that we are able to have many of the freedoms that we have now. What do you say to, really the world, who's listening about the sacrifices not only that Aaron made, but all of our men and women in uniform make?

Mrs. Vaughn: I say pray for our military every day, hold them up to the Lord and support them in any way that you can. Pray for their families, because the wives and the children are the ones that—they really have to be brave, because when their husband goes away, they don't know if he's coming back or not, and this time Aaron didn't.

CNN: Mrs. Vaughn, are you going to be heading to Dover?

Mrs. Vaughn: Pardon me?

CNN: Are you going to head to Dover?

Mrs. Vaughn: To Dover?

CNN: Yeah, do you know where they're going? I would think that...

Mrs. Vaughn: Oh, yes. We're all going when his body comes back.

CNN: Okay. Mrs. Vaughn, our thoughts and prayers really go out to you, and we thank you for being able to come on tonight and say kind words about your grandson and our men and women in uniform. Stay safe, and God bless you, okay? Thank you.

Mrs. Vaughn: Thank you.

Toward the end of the interview, I pointed up to the monitor and told the lady sitting next to me, "That's my son up there."

She said a prayer for me, and then shared the news with several others sitting nearby. Soon, a group of people had gathered around me. I wish I could personally say "thank you" to all those folks who saw me through that moment.

I flew overnight on Alaska Airlines back home. My wife and son-in-law met me at the airport. I had been up all night, and we were very casually dressed, but it was Sunday morning, and I felt the need for us to worship the Lord in the midst of our great loss. As we entered the doors of the school auditorium—our churches' makeshift sanctuary—the congregation had already begun singing, "How Great Thou Art."

After all we had been through, we felt it was important for us to remember the Lord had also been with Aaron his entire life, and this was no time to allow a root of bitterness to take hold in any of us. Gratefully, to this day, our entire family has been able to cling to our faith and embrace God's comfort in the midst of such pain.

Over the next few days, we were overwhelmed with the outpouring of love for Aaron and his fellow fallen warriors. On Sunday night, Karen, Ana, Tara and our son-in-law Adam, their two daughters, and I arrived in Virginia to be with Aaron's wife and kids. Arrangements had been made for us to stay in a house across the street from Kimberly's parents.

On Monday morning, August 8, we walked across the street to Kimberly's house. This was the very first time we were able to see her since Aaron's death. After a brief, tearful embrace, we climbed in a waiting limo to head toward our appearance on the "Today" show. NBC had contacted us the day before to set up an interview with Matt Lauer.

We arrived at the satellite location in Virginia, and the three of us spoke to Matt on the air over a video feed. As I answered my first question, Kimberly reached over and grabbed my hand. She did the same with my wife as Karen began to speak. As sensitive as we were in those moments—without any time to process or come to grips with what had happened, how it happened, and why—the interview was very emotional for us all:[2]

Matt: Kimberly Vaughn's husband, Aaron, was one of the Navy SEALs who died in that attack. She's with us now, along with Aaron's parents, Billy and Karen Vaughn. And as I welcome you to the show, please accept my condolences.

Kimberly, Karen and Billy: Thank you.

Matt: Kimberly, even as I express my condolences to you, and Mr. and Mrs. Vaughn, I was reading last night that you think we should start by making sure that our condolences are expressed to *all* the families who are grieving this morning because Aaron truly felt he was a member of the team.

Kimberly: Exactly. Although I'm able to be here this morning, and I'm thankful to share Aaron's story, the other people have also lost their loved ones and they're feeling no less grief than I am.

Matt: Mr. Vaughn, I was reading about your son and, boy, he was an impressive young man as a child, as a young adult, as a son, as a father, as a husband. He was a young man who stood out. Why did he want to be a SEAL?

Billy: Matt, I can just tell you that, after 9/11, Aaron told me and his mother that he wanted to be a SEAL, and he said that he had wanted to ever since he was a little boy. And Aaron, if I can just say it, God bless him, he loved his country, he loved God, he loved Kimberly, and he loved [his son] and [his daughter], and he honestly believed and saw black and white that what we were involved in, and he told me this, is a war for survival of our republic. Aaron knows that the war with Islamic fundamentalism, radicalism has gone on for hundreds of years...and it can be traced through history. And he felt, and so did the other members of his team, felt that the very existence of our republic is at stake. And because of that, Aaron was willing to give his life. And what I have to say is that SEAL Team VI, I just know those men felt the same way, and they see it clearly, they see it black and white. And so many of us don't, and Aaron told me right out of his own mouth that he had a class where he said, "Dad, there's three kinds – the man told us there are three kinds of people in the world, sheep dogs, sheep and wolves." And I can honestly say that SEAL Team VI are the sheep dogs. The sheep dogs always see the warning, they see it black and white, they see it clearly. The sheep, most of us are sheep. We don't usually see it.

Matt: Karen...

Billy: ...and there are some wolves out there.

Matt: Go ahead, sir, I'm sorry.

Billy: There are wolves out there, and Aaron explained it to me. And, you know, it's really strange, Matt, that ninety some odd days ago SEAL Team VI had a big victory and possibly sheep in high places said things that made *many* of us very uncomfortable. And now some ninety odd days later, SEAL Team VI has suffered a *terrible* tragedy. I just pray that during these *last* days, these next days, they'll allow SEAL Team VI, the wives, the children, the families to grieve, to bury their dead and not make it political. Just give us some time.

Matt: Karen, you said something over the weekend that really struck me. You said, now, if there is anything good to come out of this, [it is that] for the first time you get to *talk* about the amazing things that Aaron did in his life and his career with the SEALs because there's a huge code of secrecy here and now you get to brag a little about him. What are you most proud of in terms of his accomplishments?

Karen: Well [deep sigh], I'm most proud of Aaron's humility and his nobility. But more than anything, I'm most proud of the way he loved God and how important his faith was to him. And you know, Aaron, everything he did, like you said, was secret, and it just feels really strange right now, that only in his death can we celebrate who he was in his life. It's a very difficult concept to understand. But what Aaron would want everybody to know most is that he loved America, he believed America could be great again, and he fought for the America he grew up in, Matt, and we believe—we're a very patriotic family, we believe that America will be on its feet again, and a country that the rest of the world looks to as a leader. And we're just really sad about this huge loss. We're really sad that our son is gone, but we know that he would have done it all again—and he loved every minute of his life.

Matt: Kimberly, you met Aaron in Guam. I think he was serving there. You were there as a part of a USO tour, you were a member of the

Washington Redskins Cheerleaders and here was this tough warrior, but you saw a tender side of him. You have two children, [your son] is two, I believe, and your daughter was born only eight weeks ago. He made it home for both of those births. So he was home just in June. What was that visit like?

Kimberly: It was wonderful. As much as these men are gone away from their families, over hundreds of days over the years, that we make the most of our time together, and we were blessed that we could be together for the birth of our children. Aaron was an amazing father. And I'm proud that I will get to carry on his legacy through our children.

Matt: What do you want your kids to know about him when they get old enough to understand who he was, what's the one thing you want them to take away?

Kimberly: They will take away his love for Christ. They will take away his strength and his love for this country—and they will know what an amazing man he is—was.

Matt: Karen and Billy and Kimberly, thank you so much. I know how difficult it is for you to join us this morning. Please accept our condolences. And we thank Aaron for his service to this country and you for your sacrifices.

When we returned to Kimberly's parents' home, she was talking to more people from the press. Members of the military were staying by her side. While I was there, a call came in and someone on the phone wanted to talk to me. The man on the line said he was from the Navy and was worried about potential leaks of information. My mother and father, who had come in from Tennessee, were also at the house.

Earlier I had learned that someone from the Navy already spoke to my mom about her interview on CNN and had expressed concern that she had spoken publicly about the death of her grandson. In fact, my grieving mother had been basically told that if anything happened to any other Navy SEAL, based on the interview she had "leaked" to CNN, she might be to blame. You can only imagine the unnecessary and added stress this put on a lady who had just lost her beloved first-born grandson.

Understandably, the Navy was trying to take control of the situation. They didn't want the name of Navy SEAL Team VI discussed so openly.

But the news was already out. It *had* been for three months.

It was impossible to reverse.

It was then I realized how ridiculous this entire situation was becoming. The government was trying to hold the families of the Navy SEALs to a higher standard than the standard they held for themselves.

I asked this man, "What did we say that we shouldn't have said?"

"You haven't said anything wrong," he told me. "You've been doing a good job so far." I took that to mean that the "good job" included not just me, but also my mother, Kimberly, and Karen.

At that point, I had to speak up because Vice President Joe Biden had already exposed my son and other Navy SEAL Team members three months before that time. "Look," I said, "the security leaks are *not* coming from my house—they are coming from the White House. If that's the way you operate, then you need to let family members know about the protocol."

If people were not up-to-date with what Karen and I had been through for the three months prior to that day, they might be confused at my negative reaction to some questions on the "Today" show and the phone call with the Navy. What did I mean about the leaks "coming from the White House?"

To put things in context, the tremendous irony to all of this was that prior to the take down of Osama bin Laden, no one who did not need to know was aware that this particular SEAL Team even existed. Karen and I wanted to share everything we loved about Aaron with the world, but were struggling with being asked to speak in public about him. When he was alive, it was something we could never, and *would* never do in order to protect his life.

Apparently, our government did not share the same level of concern for his personal security.

3

High-Price Politics

Professing themselves to be wise,
they became fools.

- Romans 1:22 KJV

The timeline below exposes what we believe to be criminal acts against our elusive Special Operators:

May 1, 2011 — On orders, American Special Operators find and eliminate Osama bin Laden.

May 1, 2011 — President Obama gives a speech announcing the demise of Osama bin Laden.[1]

May 3, 2011 — Vice President Joe Biden makes a speech revealing the Navy SEALs were employed during the raid and Bin Laden take-down in Pakistan.[2]

May 4, 2011 — Aaron calls my wife Karen, deeply concerned about the safety of our entire family due to the outing of the Navy SEALs by Vice President Joe Biden.

May 6, 2011 — Vice President Biden, Brigadier General Jeffrey Colt, and President Obama speak at Fort Campbell. Joe Biden again elaborates about the Navy SEALs and their role in the take down of OBL. The president mentions meeting the Spec Ops team that day, but calls them "silent professionals" and notes, "success demands secrecy."[3]

May 6, 2011 — The Taliban vows revenge for the death of Osama bin Laden.

"The blood of the holy warrior sheik, Osama bin Laden, God bless him, is too precious to us and to all Muslims to go in vain," the statement said. "We will remain, God willing, a curse chasing the Americans and their agents, following them outside and inside their countries."[4]

May 11, 2011 — Data collected from official investigation of the shoot-down of *Extortion 17* reveals that more than one hundred Taliban insurgents are moving into the Tangi Valley. According to the redacted files in exhibit 89 (r_EX89, Page 8):

```
The next piece of reporting that I have that fits
within that timeframe comes from May 11 [2011] and it
late May [2011].  There's no date on this.  But it's
an                              and that is going --
so it's a                    report.  It's very brief.
```

```
Again, it's out of Task Force [ (b)(1)1.4a, (b)(1)1.4c ].  And it says
something to the effect that over 100 Taliban plan to
travel from ▬▬▬ Province through Tangi Valley to
possibly shoot down the coalition force aircraft.
```

May 12, 2011 — Defense Secretary Robert Gates expresses concern about the White House leaks.[5]

Speaking at a town hall with Marines at Camp Lejeune on Thursday morning, Defense Secretary Robert Gates said the Special Forces who participated in the successful mission to kill Osama bin Laden were *worried about their safety*, and that he was concerned that so many details of the operation had become known to the public:

"Frankly, a week ago Sunday, in the Situation Room, we all agreed that we would not release any operational details from the effort to take out bin Laden," Gates said. "That all fell apart on Monday—the next day." Gates' response was prompted by a question from a Marine in a Medical Logistics Company, who asked "what measures are being taken to protect the identities and the lives of the SEAL team members, as well as the lives of military forces deployed that might have to face extreme retaliation from terrorist organizations that want to have those identities known?"

Gates said that "there is an awareness that the threat of retaliation is increased because...of the action against bin Laden." He said there "has been a consistent and effective effort to protect the identities of those who participated in the raid, and I think that has to continue."

The defense secretary said that "when I met with the team last Thursday, they expressed a concern about that, and particularly with respect to their families...I can't get into the details in this forum, but we are looking at what measures can be taken to pump up the security."

Asked for further clarification of Gates' remarks, Pentagon press secretary Geoff Morrell said that Secretary Gates was "not pointing fingers at any particular individual or any particular building" for details becoming known. "But all of a sudden airwaves and newspapers were filled with details about a covert military and intelligence operation and that's concerning because one of the reasons that these operations—and this operation in particular—are effective is because how they do their work, how they're equipped, how they're trained, their tactics and procedures are all secret. The more that's in the public domain the less likely we'll be able to pull these operations off in the future."[6]

June 24, 2011 (Aaron Vaughn's thirtieth birthday) — CIA Director Leon Panetta leaks the name of the SEAL unit that carried out the Bin Laden raid. Panetta's leak was concealed by higher powers until after his retirement.

Former CIA Director Leon Panetta revealed the name of the Navy SEAL unit that carried out the Osama bin Laden raid and named the unit's ground commander at a 2011 ceremony attended by *Zero Dark Thirty* filmmaker Mark Boal.

Panetta also discussed classified information designated as "top secret" and "secret" during his presentation at the awards ceremony, according to a draft Pentagon inspector general's report published Wednesday by the Project on Government Oversight. The Inspector General was instructed to protect Panetta from the repercussions of this until after his retirement.7

July 20, 2011 — Taliban members make good on their promise of attempted revenge. According to the redacted files (r_ENCL B, page 7):

███████████████ Seventeen days prior to the shoot-down of EXTORTION 17, another MH-47G was engaged by small arms fire and two RPGs, and reported small caliber bullet damage to the aircraft.45 These surface-to-air fire events indicated insurgent capability and intent to engage coalition forces aircraft operating in the Tangi Valley.46

August 6, 2011 — Taliban and al-Qaeda forces shoot down *Extortion 17*, carrying seventeen Navy SEALs with five additional support staff to SEAL Team VI. In total, thirty Americans, one dog and eight Afghans die.

Aaron served his nation proudly and felt that he was making a difference. But in the last year and a half of his life, he began to grow leery of the direction he and his fellow SEALs were being led.

Things had changed overseas. The menacing Taliban rulers had been run out of Afghanistan and Saddam Hussein and his statue had been toppled; no longer towering over Iraq and its people. The proud blue thumbs-ups in both nations were a sign that the Afghanis and Iraqis were free to vote in their own governments. Even so, our forces serving in

Afghanistan, where my boy was deployed during 2010, had to a take a very defensive posture.

I remember on one of Aaron's visits home, less than a year before his death, he told me how careful they needed to be in order to ensure their own safety—expressing his lack of trust in working alongside the Afghanis. He told us that no Afghanis were given any information on their operations.

He actually said, "We don't tell them [Afghanis] where we're going until we get there, because if we do, the enemy [the Taliban] will be ready for us when we show up." He also said, "We can't trust them. They stand there and let us fight."

He and his teammates had found out the hard way that trust was not a luxury they could afford. On more than one operation, his team had been abandoned by the Afghanis, left to carry a weight heavier than planned, creating undue danger.

Honestly, what I did not and still do not understand was why highly trained Special Forces—prepared to carry out elite operations and play a very specific and secretive role—were being exposed to and were training the Afghanis.

But what haunts me most since his death are these words, spoken in a father-son conversation about his presumed ally, "Dad, they are only loyal to the highest bidder."

It was back on May 1, 2011, that a call came from Aaron. His voice sounded elated as he exclaimed, "Dad, we got him!"

"Got who, son?" I asked.

"Who do you think? Go turn on the TV."

The Navy SEALs had done what should have been done two administrations ago under Bill Clinton: they took out Osama bin Laden. But I would like to point out here that Aaron *never* said, "the SEALs." Aaron was very tight-lipped about these things—his first priority was always to protect his brothers.

In his voice I heard the peace my son felt, knowing his team had finally downed the monster that ordered the murder of so many Americans and wreaked so much havoc on our nation.

I turned on the news. President Obama soon took to the podium and delivered his speech—that infamous speech covered by all major networks—declaring to our nation that Osama bin Laden was, in fact, dead.

I have included part of the president's speech below. Halfway through, I jokingly wondered to myself if Aaron had heard it wrong. It sounded to me as if the president himself had taken out Bin Laden:[8]

> ...And so shortly after taking office, I directed Leon Panetta, the director of the CIA, to make the killing or capture of bin Laden the top priority of our war against al Qaeda, even as we continued our broader efforts to disrupt, dismantle, and defeat his network. Then, last August, after years of painstaking work by our intelligence community, I was briefed on a possible lead to bin Laden. It was far from certain, and it took many months to run this thread to ground. I met repeatedly with my national security team as we developed more information about the possibility that we had located bin Laden hiding within a compound deep inside of Pakistan. And finally, last week, I determined that we had enough intelligence to take action, and authorized

an operation to get Osama bin Laden and bring him to justice.

Today, at my direction, the United States launched a targeted operation against that compound in Abbottabad, Pakistan. A small team of Americans carried out the operation with extraordinary courage and capability. No Americans were harmed. They took care to avoid civilian casualties. After a firefight, they killed Osama bin Laden and took custody of his body.

For over two decades, bin Laden has been al Qaeda's leader and symbol, and has continued to plot attacks against our country and our friends and allies. The death of bin Laden marks the most significant achievement to date in our nation's effort to defeat al Qaeda.

Yet his death does not mark the end of our effort. There is no doubt that al Qaeda will continue to pursue attacks against us. We must -- and we will -- remain vigilant at home and abroad.

As we do, we must also reaffirm that the United States is not -- and never will be -- at war with Islam. I've made clear, just as President Bush did shortly after 9/11, that our war is not against Islam. Bin Laden was not a Muslim leader; he was a mass murderer of Muslims. Indeed, al Qaeda has slaughtered scores of Muslims in many countries, including our own. So his demise should be welcomed by all who believe in peace and human dignity.

Over the years, I have repeatedly made clear that we would take action within Pakistan if we knew where bin

Laden was. That is what we have done. But it is important to note that our counterterrorism cooperation with Pakistan helped lead us to bin Laden and the compound where he was hiding. Indeed, bin Laden had declared war against Pakistan as well, and ordered attacks against the Pakistani people.

Tonight, I called President Zardari, and my team has also spoken with their Pakistani counterparts. They agree that this is a good and historic day for both of our nations. And going forward, it is essential that Pakistan continue to join us in the fight against al Qaeda and its affiliates.

The American people did not choose this fight. It came to our shores, and started with the senseless slaughter of our citizens. After nearly ten years of service, struggle, and sacrifice, we know well the costs of war. These efforts weigh on me every time I, as Commander-in-Chief, have to sign a letter to a family that has lost a loved one, or look into the eyes of a service member who's been gravely wounded.

So Americans understand the costs of war. Yet as a country, we will never tolerate our security being threatened, nor stand idly by when our people have been killed. We will be relentless in defense of our citizens and our friends and allies. We will be true to the values that make us who we are. And on nights like this one, we can say to those families who have lost loved ones to al Qaeda's terror: Justice has been done.

Each "I" became a punch in the gut as I could only imagine what the SEALs involved had gone through and the danger that engulfed them. How could I help being outraged at the president's pointed referrals to himself in the speech? "*I* directed...*I* was briefed...*I* met repeatedly with my national security...*I* determined...at *my* direction...*I* made it clear..."

But then I laughed at how ridiculous he was being. The pathetic attention the president brought to himself was exactly the opposite of what the SEALs would do regarding their work. His speech made something vividly clear to me—the president, and for that matter those in the White House—would *never* understand a Navy SEAL.

Eventually, the image of the situation room during the raid was released and when a mock image followed with Obama's head imposed on every body, I knew I wasn't the only one who found his self-congratulatory victory speech nauseating. But on that night, along with everyone in the nation, as an American, I was relieved and happy.

As a father, I was so proud of the Navy SEALs and thrilled for Aaron that he and his buddies could share this monumental victory. I knew it was an endeavor our Intelligence Community and the Navy SEALs had been diligently pursuing long before President Obama took office. As the parent of a SEAL, I was satisfied with just being quietly proud.

But within a day, my pride and joy turned to shock and anger when Vice President Joe Biden took to the stage at a black tie dinner at Washington's Ritz Carlton Hotel to mark the 50th anniversary of the Atlantic Council. Here are excerpts from Biden's speech:[9]

> Let me briefly acknowledge tonight's distinguished honorees. Admiral James Stavridis is the real deal. He can tell you more about and understands the incredible, the phenomenal, the just almost unbelievable capacity of his

Navy SEALs and what they did last Sunday...Folks, I'd be remiss also if I didn't say an extra word about the incredible events, extraordinary events of this past Sunday. As Vice President of the United States, as an American, I was in absolute awe of the capacity and dedication of the entire team, both the intelligence community, the CIA, the SEALs. It just was extraordinary.

My wife and I were stunned. When we saw the news reports, we could not believe the *Vice President* of the United States had openly breached national security by confirming to the world that the Navy SEALs had, in fact, been the team who took down Osama bin Laden.

Less than twenty-four hours later, Aaron called Karen and his voice was very concerned. "Mom, listen to me, you have to wash your social media clean right now. Wipe everything off of it," Aaron said, "There's chatter and all of our lives are in danger including yours, Mom."

Then, within a week of the raid on Bin Laden's compound, Obama granted unprecedented access to Kathryn Bigelow, the Academy Award®[10] winning director of *The Hurt Locker,* and screenwriter Mark Boal for the rights to make a movie on the killing of Osama bin Laden. The movie *Zero Dark Thirty* was originally intended to come out in theaters just before the 2012 election, but it was delayed.

Then emails were released showing just how much access the Hollywood group was given: "Rep. Peter King (R-N.Y.), chairman of the House Committee on Homeland Security, said in a statement Wednesday that the emails tell a 'damning story of extremely close, unprecedented, and potentially dangerous collaboration' with top officials at the CIA, Department of Defense and the White House, as well as with a top Democratic lobbying firm, the Glover Park Group."[11]

To us, this was pure madness. The Obama Administration was politically manipulating the US military for its own selfish gain at the expense of our elite forces and our national security.

Then, there we stood on August 6th, just three months after that devastating betrayal, and Aaron was dead. Biden and Panetta had exposed the SEALs. Biden was endlessly praising Obama for his *brave* decision.

Obama was making a movie.

So as Karen and I sat that day on August 8, 2011, after our son died, preparing to speak with Matt Lauer, we were both still in a state of shock, wondering what exactly *we* could say about our son—the son we had never been able to speak about before in order to secure his safety. In a heart-wrenching moment of clarity we realized—the damage had already been done.

There was nothing left to protect.

As I look back now and think of what I said to Matt Lauer about not wanting this incident to be politicized, I can understand that if someone didn't know me, if they had no clue where I was coming from, they may think I was the one politicizing the event of my son's death. Especially by calling out Joe Biden. But from my perspective, I was simply asking the White House not to use *our* current tragedy for political points, like they had with the Bin Laden take down.

Ninety-three days earlier my boy told us he had become a target at the hands of his Commander-in-Chief, and now he was dead.

I was angry, hurt and confused. It was nearly impossible to process my thoughts without wondering if Biden's comments and the president's Hollywood dreams may have cost us our only son.

But now, in the midst of all our emotions and questions, *we* were being told that *we* needed to be quiet? The Navy was concerned about what *we* might say? The whole thing felt ridiculous. *We* had the real concerns. *We* deserved answers, yet the tables were being turned on us. Most especially, I could not believe the fact that someone had intimidated my mother in the midst of our tragedy. I felt like I was in another world. The whole situation was not making any sense.

As that day dragged on, we gathered at Kimberly's parents' house. My family wanted to comfort Kimberly during this difficult time, but due to the military personnel present and protocols that we were asked to follow, for the most part we were separated from her and our grandchildren. I felt like we were being "handled." But out of respect for the Navy and the military that Aaron loved and fought with, we all did our best to cooperate. It was tough not being able to grieve privately as a family.

Watching the news unfold that afternoon, we learned that a National Guard chopper had been used to fly the Navy SEALs and other Special Operations warriors into that fatal mission. As we watched the broadcast, one of Aaron's buddies sitting near me made a statement I vividly remember.

He said, "This mission was [f'ed] up from the very beginning."

Although this comment raised a dark red flag in my mind, it would be much, much later before I'd learn the true depth of his heartbreaking statement.

4

Pomp and Circumstance

*When the righteous thrive, the people
rejoice; when the wicked rule,
the people groan.*

- Proverbs 29:2 NIV

On the night before receiving Aaron's body in Dover, Delaware, a member of the Navy approached Karen and me in person. He asked if we had a preference regarding the presence of media or photographers at the upcoming ceremony. He told us they were asking all the families for their feedback. We politely declined both. We said absolutely no press coverage, absolutely no pictures; this event was going to be difficult enough.

We wanted to receive our son privately.

We were told nineteen of the thirty families felt the same.

On Tuesday morning, August 9th, the military loaded all the families onto buses and drove us to Dover Air Force Base. When we arrived, we were guided into a big receiving area—like a large ballroom, but sectioned off by family groups. Each family was assigned a representative from the branch of service in which their son had served.

While we waited to receive the caskets, there was a buffet of food set out for us. Eventually, military dignitaries arrived to meet all the families. President Obama was there, as was the Secretary of Defense Leon Panetta, Chairman of the Joint Chiefs of Staff Admiral Mike Mullen, and many others. Vice President Joe Biden did not attend. Every dignitary took the time to speak with each group, offering condolences to each person present. The government had gone out of its way to accommodate all the families that morning.

Most notably in attendance were Navy SEAL operators who had probably flown all night to Dover for the ceremony. They were standing by their brothers in arms while also showing honor and respect to their fallen brothers' families. This gesture meant a great deal to us, and we know it would have meant so much to Aaron.

Eventually we were put back on buses and driven to the receiving hanger—a big metal shed with no air conditioning. As we turned the corner to enter, Karen became weak and groaned in pain. On the other side of the hanger, just beyond the open doors, sat two huge C-17 military transport aircrafts loaded side-to-side and front-to-back with flag-draped coffins. I had never seen anything like it—so many in one place.

Nothing could have prepared us for this moment.

Karen later recalled that there was an enormous American flag draped from the roof beams in the center of the hanger. I don't remember seeing the flag, but she later told me that the breathtaking imagery nearly sent her to her knees. We were miserable in the August heat, and our hearts were broken.

This was real.

They were home.

A number of people, including my mother and mother-in-law, found this part physically challenging. Not surprisingly, the flood of emotions combined with the heat caused a few people to collapse. Wheelchairs were provided for those in need, and refreshments were distributed to all in attendance to help us endure the day.

The families—I'm guessing at least two hundred and fifty of us— sat in folding chairs. Members of the military sat in bleachers on the other side of the hanger, an open path between us. The caskets were ceremonially ushered in one-by-one and loaded into transport vehicles near the center of the building.

Each transport vehicle held either six or eight caskets. When a vehicle reached capacity, the doors would be shut in reverent ceremony. It would then exit at a pace so that the dignitaries, including President Obama, could walk beside it until it was fully out of sight. Another would be backed in, and the process would continue.

We noticed that eight of the thirty-eight coffins were draped with Afghan flags. Afterwards, it was explained to us that all remains from the crash had been brought to the United States so bodies could be identified through DNA and dental records. Though it didn't dawn on me at the time, I soon realized there was a high probability that some of our American soldiers—possibly even my son—returned to their native land in a casket draped with an "Islamic Republic of Afghanistan" flag. I cannot put into words the depth of anger I feel when I contemplate the possibility.

The names of the fallen were not announced. It was just a homecoming for thirty nameless American men mingled with eight Afghanis— whose flag-draped caskets were paraded in with equal ceremony to the Americans. A few questions were asked, but most of the families were too emotionally overwhelmed in that moment to challenge or question the military and President Obama on this decision.

I felt trapped between respecting the dead, being a dutiful American, and defending my son's honor. The sight of Afghan flags disturbed me greatly, but the sight was so unexpected, I wasn't sure how I was supposed to feel or what I could say. Looking back, I'm incredibly offended that military officials showed no greater respect for their fallen heroes or the heroes' families who had proudly supported their sons' service to the United States of America. I'm left pondering this thought: Are our military leaders really this calloused and naïve, or was this a calculated risk they were willing to take while seeking to build a political coalition?

Later that afternoon, back at the hotel, an official with the Navy approached me and once again expressed some concern that we were talking too much to the media. His words stung my heart, *"The Grandma went on CNN."*

It had already been a very tough morning. My emotions flared up just thinking how they had put the weight of the world on my poor, aging, grief-stricken mother. No one seemed to care that she had just lost her grandson. And here they were—scaring her with what might happen to other SEALs due to her CNN interview.

With that, I was done defending the actions of my family. I was now angry. "What do you mean *The Grandma*? She is *Aaron's* grandmother and she is *my* mother. It's funny to me that CNN could find Aaron's grandmother quicker than Naval Special Warfare did."

The man did not respond to this comment. Again, I wanted to know how Aaron's grandmother was supposed to know about the Naval Special Warfare protocol. My mother did not call CNN; CNN called her. The Navy was coming down on the grandmother of a slain SEAL, when we had no instruction on how to deal with the media. To this day, my family and I still don't know how CNN knew that Aaron was on *Extortion 17* because the names had not been released at that point.

In that same confrontation, this man also warned me that my actions "could" put a black mark on my son's name. To which I responded, "Aaron has died an honorable warrior. He's gone now. The only one who could put a black mark on his name is the United States Navy. That's *YOUR* choice."

Karen and I had agreed on Monday of that week to do a Fox News interview on Thursday morning. By Tuesday evening Naval Special Warfare (NSW) had assigned a public affairs officer to intercept the media on our behalf. Various members of the press had been approaching us, particularly Fox News, since the day after Aaron died. I told our public affairs officer that finally, after multiple requests, we had already agreed to the Thursday morning interview. She told me she "would suggest" that Karen and I not make the appearance. But I had already made a commitment, and my word is my word.

She ended the conversation with, "I'll have my public affairs liaison waiting for you at Fox News."

On Thursday, the limo came to pick us up and the public affairs liaison assigned from NSW was already at the studio. As we waited, he had a meeting behind closed doors with the people at Fox and then we went on air. We don't know what was said or agreed to during that discussion.

Here is our interview with Steve Doocy:[1]

Steve: A US airstrike has killed the Taliban insurgents whose attack caused that helicopter crash that killed thirty US servicemen in Afghanistan. Seventeen of those Navy SEALs, including Aaron Vaughn, whose faith in God and country led him to pursue service with the SEALs in the wake of September the 11th. Aaron's parents, Billy and Karen Vaughn join us live right now from Washington, DC. Good morning to you.

Karen: Good morning. Thank you, Steve, for having us.

Billy: Good morning.

Steve: Listen, thank you. I know that you have had just the worst week possible, and for you to join us today, says a lot about you. Because I know you want to talk about your son, and we just put up his picture. Tell us about Aaron.

Billy: Aaron was the boy that any mom and dad could dream of having. Just a pleasure to raise: lots of joy, little bit of aggravation [everyone chuckles], lots of fun, lots of laughs.

Karen: That's what I would say most about Aaron, we've been talking as a family, the biggest thing that is gonna hurt about him being gone is he was just bigger than life. And he was just always fun. Every time he came home it was, "hey, y'all watch this" moments, and we all just had a blast every time he was around. He made sure, you know?

Steve: We just showed a picture of your son, you're holding him as a little boy, wearing camo. This job as a Navy SEAL is something that he has wanted since he was little.

Karen: Yes, yes. Yeah, from the time...his father has the story about the day he realized what a Navy SEAL was. I'll let him tell that.

Billy: Yeah, when Aaron was growing up and when I was a lot younger, we lived on a farm there in Tennessee, Northwest Tennessee, and a lot of times on Saturdays would be out together working on the farm or doing something. And one day something came up on the radio in the truck about the Army Rangers. Aaron didn't tell me this story until after he had become a SEAL. Something came on about the Army Rangers, and he listened to it, and I told him, I said, "Son, there is a group that may be just possibly a notch above that, cause they go in water, and they do things and they come from the air, and they do those things like that..." The story was never repeated after our conversation after one time when Aaron came home and, "Dad" and I didn't remember it, he had remembered every bit of it, and he said, "Dad, ever since you and I were in the truck when you were riding down the road by the Wade place when you told me about that, that's what I've wanted to be."

Steve: And his dream came true; he became a Navy SEAL.

Billy: He did.

Karen: He did.

Steve: And he served proudly. We just led this segment with the news that apparently the people who brought down that chopper with the RPGs, apparently we've had an attack and they are all dead. Does that help?

Karen: Help? No. Feel good, yes.

Billy: Yeah, that's what it's all about. I mean, and our son and the rest of them I'm sure would, that's what they were after.

Steve: There had been some suggestion that perhaps this attack on that helicopter was payback for the Bin Laden raid, Bin Laden, of course, responsible for September the 11th. September the 11th really changed Aaron's life. That was one of the things that really motivated him to become a member of the US military, wasn't it?

Billy: That's right because in high school Aaron had torn his ACL and it had ruined his playing football, which was where his heart was when he was in high school. And so he couldn't play any sports or if he did after that, in any kind of amateur sports, playing basketball or football on Saturdays with boys and stuff like that, he always had to wear a knee brace. And then he came in after 9/11, on his twenty-first birthday. He had already gotten a degree, and he was pursuing another career, and he came in on his twenty-first birthday and sat us down at the table that night and told us what he had done. That he had joined and wanted to be a SEAL. Then he had to become a SEAL and he had to train as a SEAL without his knee brace because he couldn't let anybody know he didn't have an ACL.

Karen: He was remarkable.

Steve: That *is* remarkable. I know that they brought his body back a couple of days ago to Dover, and because nineteen of thirty families objected, there were not supposed to be any pictures taken, and none were by anybody except the White House. And the White House did release a picture. In fact, they made it the picture of the day of the President of the United States saluting at some of the caskets, as some of the bodies were brought off the airplane. Do you feel it's appropriate that the White House released those, that particular picture, even though there were objections from so many families?

Billy: Let me ask you Steve, are you surprised?

Steve: I am surprised given the fact the Pentagon said there would be absolutely no images, that, and then there was an image. That did surprise me.

Karen: It's disappointing.

Billy: It is very disappointing.

Steve: Yeah.

Billy: In fact, we were impressed that the president was there with no press. We were impressed about that...that's what impressed us. There was no press as far as we were told, and then this.

Steve: Well, I know at this point, funeral plans are uncertain, because you don't know exactly when you are going to get the body of your son. But you are going to have a memorial service. Tell us a little bit about that.

Karen: Well, Aaron, he grew up in a small town in West Tennessee, and you know he's just their hometown hero; those people love him. We moved to Florida when he was sixteen years old, but he actually went back to that high school in Tennessee to graduate because those people were his family and the people he grew up with and loved in the community. And so it was a fitting place to have his first memorial, and Billy and I talked to [Aaron's] wife about it, and she was 100 percent, you know, ready to do it, so we went ahead and planned it. The family is working their tails off right now to put it all together. To pay honor to Aaron the way everybody wants to.

Steve: Absolutely.

Billy: But we would like to say that he has some very dear friends in Florida. *Very* dear friends who have made a *very* big impact on his life and changed him a lot as a young man growing up.

Steve: Well, you know what, Karen and Billy? He has got a lot of new friends all across this country looking in, and we thank you so much for joining us today to tell to us about your son Aaron.

Billy: I tell you Steve, he's got friends in heaven that we've never seen. And we know he's there with the Lord now, and we know he could not have left this world without it being the Lord's will, and we're good with that.

Steve: Billy and Karen, thank you so much for joining us on such a tough week.

Karen and Billy: Thank you.

Steve: Our thoughts and prayers are with you and your family.

Karen and Billy: Thanks.

August 9, 2011 Photo of the Day with President Obama and Defense Secretary Panetta: "President Barack Obama, in the process of saluting, participates in a ceremony at Dover Air Force Base in Dover, Del., Aug. 9, 2011, for the dignified transfer of U.S. and Afghan personnel who died in Afghanistan on Aug. 6. (Official White House Photo by Pete Souza)"[2]

We'd been told directly that, based on the overwhelming majority of family responses, there would be *no* press or photographs at Dover AFB. But there, during our interview, on the screen at Fox News, was an image Karen and I were seeing for the first time. It was a perfectly posed photo of President Obama saluting the caskets, specifically designed to show the president in the best light. That's when Steve Doocy asked me,

"Do you feel it's appropriate that the White House released those, that particular picture, even though there were objections from so many families?"

I wasn't surprised or even shocked that the death of these warriors was being used as political capital for the president while at the same time, my family and I were being put under pressure by Naval Special Warfare to not be political. So I just asked him, "Steve, are you surprised?"

Soon after the interview on Fox News, the public affairs officer from San Diego's Naval Special Warfare called me and said, "You did a good job, but when Steve Doocy mentioned the president and the photographs, you rolled your eyes, and you *CAN'T* do that. You *CAN'T* make this political." I look back on that moment now and believe wholeheartedly that Karen and I did our best under such emotional pressure, especially knowing that three months earlier, Vice President Joe Biden had committed a breach of national security by leaking confidential information to the world, and particularly to our enemies, that the Navy SEALs brought down Osama bin Laden. Joe Biden put a target on my son's back.

What the Navy was asking us to do was to control *our* emotions, two grieving parents who just lost their only son. My heart was too heavy to play political games, but *I* was being asked to be a politician: *no* emotion, *no* real feeling. We were outraged that President Obama, with gross disrespect for the wishes of the majority of the grieving families, was once again using SEAL Team VI for political gain. Had he not done enough? In a roundabout and absurd way, the Navy and the White House administration expected us to be a part of a cover-up, when our questions were only emerging.

The irony, in my mind, was when the public affairs officer from San Diego's NSW told Karen and me not to be political, when they were themselves being political. In fact, the president and vice president had been full-on political for three months, saying whatever they wanted. But now they were suppressing *our* real feelings about our son's death by pressuring us with their agenda. They wanted us silenced.

On August 24th we were once again flown to Virginia Beach, this time for the Naval Special Warfare Development Group (DEVGRU) memorial service at the Virginia Beach Convention Center. Most of our family was in attendance as well as several close friends. There must have been two entire ships full of sailors lining the streets leading up to the Convention Center, all dressed in their sharply pressed uniforms, all standing at complete attention, each one saluting us and the other families as we made our way through the crowds in buses chartered by the military.

It was an *overwhelming* sight to behold.

Even though twenty days had passed since Aaron died, I think we were still in a state of shock, but between the sights, the sounds, and outpouring of support, just as we felt at the first sight of the caskets at Dover, we were able to carry on and get through the day. Again, all the families somehow had to find a way to balance tremendous pain with an equal amount of pride in the honor being paid to our sons.

The next day, following the conclusion of the ceremony honoring all the fallen heroes of *Extortion 17*, we continued with a flight from Virginia Beach to Reagan National Airport to attend a chapel service held at Arlington National Cemetery. More words were spoken and more prayers were offered. We then witnessed our son's casket, along with twelve others who were on *Extortion 17,* being laid to rest among the countless other American heroes who had given their lives for our nation.

After the service, in anticipation of the landfall of Hurricane Irene, the families were rushed by airplane back to Virginia Beach. There, we were grounded for the weekend with an ocean view from our hotel, surrounded with survival supplies we had purchased from a local Kmart. Ana, Tara, Adam, and their two children stayed in their own rooms in the same hotel, and when it was safe to leave, they all flew back to Florida. Tara's oldest daughter Belle, our first grandchild, was very close to her "Uncle Aaron." She had expressed a lot of anguish over his death. But Tara's youngest daughter, Lyla, hadn't said much at all through this entire process, nor had she cried. During their long, quiet flight home, Tara held Lyla in her lap, as she sat staring out the window, tears flowing down her cheeks. Finally, little Lyla, just under three years old, spoke with genuine curiosity:

"Why are you crying?"

"Because I'm sad about Uncle Aaron." She was choking back tears.

"I saw him last night, Mom," Lyla said, with a matter-of-fact attitude—no different than if she'd just seen him at the local grocery.

Jolted by the words, Tara asked, "Where, honey?"

"In heaven."

"What was he doing?" Tara, now overcome with emotion, was very careful about not putting any words in Lyla's mouth.

"He was riding a horse, and Mom, he's doing just fine," again, with that matter-of-fact attitude.

This was the first time she had spoken of him since his death three weeks prior. About two weeks later, she brought up the same story and repeated it again, but this time she added:

"Mom, he was doing 'the hut, hut.'"

"What do you mean 'the hut, hut'?"

"You know, 'the hut, hut', when the men say, hut...hut...hut..." Tara took this to mean Aaron was in training for a bigger battle than any he had known here on earth.

After the storm subsided, Karen and I, along with my mom and dad, rented a car and drove to West Tennessee. We had another family funeral to attend. While at Arlington, for Aaron's burial on August 26th, I had been notified that my cousin, Ben Carson Vaughn, had died of health complications due to his long-term battle with brain cancer. When Carson was a young man, he was often at our house in West Tennessee. Aaron was a little boy back then. It was surreal for me to acknowledge that both of them were gone, both still so young. Karen and I had such wonderful memories of them playing together in our home during our early family life.

After an exhausting few weeks, we flew back home. Karen had the window seat on the airplane. The sun was descending, yet radiant enough to enjoy the incredible sky. She was gazing out the window when she said to me, "Oh my gosh! Look at this."

There, Karen and I witnessed a sight that honestly astounded us, and still does to this day. Four different clouds, all right next to each other, spelled out the word:

"H-O-M-E"

We accepted this as a gift from the Lord, reassuring us that Aaron was indeed, safely home. It was such a comfort and blessing.

In September, after all the memorial services were over, Karen and I went to visit Kimberly. While on that trip I made an appointment to meet with a high-ranking Naval Special Warfare Officer at DEVGRU Command. My purpose for going there was that I knew something unsettling was wrong with that mission. As it was stated numerous times on TV, the thirty American warriors were flying in a chopper that should not have been used for Special Operations. Therefore, I had some questions that I wanted answered. I was welcomed at the Command center, and during that visit I learned three key things. These three things did nothing to bring me peace, they just increased my concern about the lack of leadership in the wars in Iraq and Afghanistan. Here is how my conservation went:

Billy: Were the men really on a CH-47D Chinook?

NSW Officer: Yes.

Billy: Why were they on the CH-47?

NSW Officer: I was told that a MH-47 was not used because it was not available.

Billy: Why was a MH-47 not available?

NSW Officer: Because our country is not engaged in this war.

What I believe this DEVGRU member meant was our citizenry are living like our men are not fighting, therefore our men in battle do not have the equipment they need.

Billy: If they had been in a MH-47 instead of a CH-47, would the results have been the same?

NSW Officer: I can tell you this, if the chopper had been hit in the same place, the results would have been the same. But what we'll never know is this: if they'd been in the MH-47, would they have been hit at all? In the MH-47, they would have had different pilots, they would have gone in a lot faster, and would have probably gone in at a different angle.

I took that to mean that the Army Special Operations choppers were not only faster, but certainly better equipped for evasive and defensive maneuvers. Finally, I was left with this very haunting statement:

NSW Officer: Just because you do something wrong a thousand times and get away with it, it doesn't make it right.

This was an indication to me that the DEVGRU team members had a view that we were operating in a way that was dangerous and reckless. So what was it that had been done wrong a thousand times? And were those wrongs still happening in theater today? What other mistakes, errors, or just flat-out bad decisions were taking place in this war, putting our men and women in grave and unnecessary danger?

5

Death of a Team Guy

The Lord said, "What have you done?
Listen! Your brother's blood cries out to me
from the ground.

- Genesis 4:10 NIV

Weeks had passed since we'd laid Aaron to rest, and yet I still felt I could not move on. I'd been trying to settle these feelings ever since Aaron's friend made that comment about the mission being "f'ed up." Even though I knew and completely understood mistakes could be made in missions, my questions were building. Of course, Aaron could never tell me much about the missions he participated in, but I couldn't help thinking about some of the very disturbing things he *had* told me.

What I did know was that with everything going on over his two previous deployments, Aaron's comfort level had been changing.

One time, Aaron described a mission to me that took place in a very remote location in Afghanistan. I believe it was up in the Hindu Kush area, around early 2010, during the cold Afghan winter. There was a Taliban stronghold where a main road went right through their village, so the SEALs went in the back way, hiking for several days. There were about six to eight SEALs, some CIA operatives, and some Afghan Commandos. I can't remember exactly how many Afghanis were with Aaron and his group, but there were more Afghanis than SEALs. They all hiked toward the Taliban carrying their gear, and in addition, the SEALs carried ladders with them to get up and down large cliffs. The Afghan Commandos carried only their own gear and did not assist with the ladders.

The mission was carefully timed so the entire Special Operation in the village could be done at night, and the SEALs route out on foot could be carried out in darkness. The exfil by the chopper would be done just before daylight or right at dawn so as not to expose the SEALs or the chopper. Because their route out was in a valley with mountains on either side, the geography made them extremely vulnerable to Taliban snipers shooting from the mountains in the daylight.

The SEALs were in the front, the Afghanis were following in the middle, and the CIA operatives were in the rear of this secret expedition. At some point the operatives contacted the SEALs and told them the Afghanis stopped, sat down, and outright refused to continue with the hike to the enemy village because they were fatigued. The Afghanis went on *strike* in the middle of the cold wilderness. At this point, the delay obviously put the entire operation in jeopardy.

When they eventually entered the village—the raid area—the Afghanis refused to fight. Furthermore, they had been delayed enough that the operation was not completed before sunup, forcing them to exit during daylight—exactly what they had planned to avoid.

As expected, they were exposed to the Taliban's bullets as they exited the valley. The SEALs called for more air support before catching a break. The Americans picked up radio correspondence from the Taliban members firing at our team in the valley, and were able to identify their position in the mountains. After hours of fighting, the SEALs overheard radio chatter that Taliban leaders in the area were calling off the attack for fear of losing all of their fighters to the Americans. According to Aaron, everyone on his team made it back alive.

Even though the mission was a success, there had been no willpower among the Afghanis to fight with the Americans, and this lack of cooperation was a drag on our men. It also changed the odds dramatically due to a heightened lack of trust. The overall absence of will by the Afghanis was a threat to our operations. It seemed to me when Aaron told me this story that our most elite warriors were now fighting two battles at once: one within the operation while they babysat the Afghanis traveling with them, and a second equally dangerous battle—fighting the Taliban.

Then again, I wonder if they were fighting a third battle as well. When Aaron came home in 2010, he handed me a sobering writing from an anonymous SEAL. I've searched the Internet, but I have not seen it published anywhere. I have no idea if Aaron or one of his buddies wrote it, but that is what I suspect. Since Aaron's death I've re-read this, and the tension I read in these lines has only added to my great and ever-growing concern for our military.

I initially asked myself in disbelief: how are our warriors being torn between their fierce love of country and the growing doubt some are experiencing about the circumstances in which they are being asked to fight? I believe the intense level of frustration shown below is the result of what's now being asked of these mighty warriors. This is the raw version from my warrior son:

Death of a Team Guy
Author Anonymous[1]

Brave men have fought and died building the proud tradition and feared reputation that I am bound to uphold. In the worst of conditions, the legacy of my teammates steadies my resolve and silently guides my every deed. I will not fail." These are the final words in the Navy SEAL code. Whether or not you agree with the "code", no SEAL can dispute those words, and no one within this community can deny that our "proud tradition" and "feared reputation" are quickly disintegrating before the entire community's eyes, and I for one will not sit idly by and remain a part of this painful transformation. The "devils with green faces" have traded their devil horns for high-and-tights and their green face paint in for shaving cream. Our community is made up of some of the toughest and smartest men in the military, but we are losing our identity and our respect day by day. Identifying the problem is easy for most of us.

The first problem, and this is obvious to any frogman, is the insatiable demand for political correctness and sensitivity within the military in general, including the sacred SEAL teams. What's most disgusting is our willingness to oblige these ludicrous demands that go against what I believe are the very core of what we are supposed to be. Once upon a time "SEAL" was feared, it meant warrior. Now it just means sailor.

Simply stated, men are turning into women not only throughout American society, but throughout our armed services as well. Our leaders have become too weak to stand tall and shoot straight. We no longer opt for the most sensible and practical approach to war, we now consider what those outside our community will think or say if we do this instead of that. The fact is that our leaders are forced to choose between what's best for the task and what is politically correct, or what is best according to? The politicians and the emasculated. Our morals have been shelved so that we may cater to those weak few who shame masculinity and preach peace & harmony. Well God forbid that the United States Military look bad in the eyes of these flag-burners, after all, if these people don't like us, who then will they ask to come on television and talk about military strategy on CNN during a war? Let's be honest here, winning the war is important, but it is nowhere near the top of the military's list. If it were, I might be writing this essay on the combat-proven effectiveness of tactical nukes in OIF or something...

Did we join the SEAL Teams to do battle for America or to add a check in the box for our personal resume? To kill terrorists or make rank? To be "squared away" or to destroy evil? Many of us are here for the wrong reasons. It isn't difficult to see who is here for the right reasons and who has their priorities straight, and it is those that are here as patriots and warriors are the men we want to lead us and follow us to no end, not the future admirals and CEOs; the difference is obvious. What kind of a warrior wants to go into battle led by a man who would rather put a bullet in his FITREP than put a bullet in the bad guy? Its men like this who have taken the SEAL teams from the most respected of outfits with unimaginable potential to just another military unit who settles for what's best for those holding the reigns, not those pulling the sled. Some guys are more excited to put the trident on their resume than on their chest. That isn't who we want making decisions for the team, but that is exactly who holds the strings, largely. I realize now that most of the great leaders in our community who the men most respect, are being flushed out of the teams faster than you can say SRB. These are the leaders that we will follow into battle with passion and pride and without remorse. What's even stranger is that these men seem to be the ones with the most heart and passion for our cause. Out of the 47 graduates from my BUD/s class, only 23 reenlisted after their first hitch, and most of these guys are the best of the bunch. But surely if they're such great men and devoted patriots they would stay and serve as long as possible, right? Not true; it's just too heart-breaking to stay and be tied down and restrained for another deployment. Then why are these great men going away? Because greed and politics are taking over, and those who fight for the men and fight for what is morally right as opposed to fight for themselves are hung out to dry and left in the dust; because they spent more time trying to write up their boys for awards and not enough time writing themselves up. Most of the guys that do stay in do so only in the interest of going to Dam Neck. The hope is that maybe Dam Neck is what we all thought the teams would be. What seems to be the most frustrating point is that everyone sees the potential of the teams, but we simply aren't fulfilling this potential. Some of the reasons for this are completely out of our hands, but most are easily within our realm to change. It's easier to stick with what has always worked. It's easier to be conventional, and that's exactly what we are, we're a really, really good conventional force. We have unarguably the most difficult and demanding training known to modern militaries, yet our standards (post BUD/S) seem to be no higher than the next group's.

The whole advancement system just plain sucks, and if something doesn't change, being a SEAL in the Navy will soon be as common as being a paratrooper in the Army. Our leaders shouldn't be evaluated and promoted based on self-written reports we know as FITREPs. In this community, we evaluate each other every day, and we should advance in rank based on the merit which is given to us by our brothers and not based on how pretty the words are on a self-descriptive brag-sheet. That is what matters. Instead, the prettiest eval gets the ticket to the next pay-grade, despite the fact that the peer consensus of who should become leaders and who should go away are near opposites to who is in fact being promoted. I hope one day I am sitting before a commanding officer at a mast because I wore black socks instead of white.

My loyalty is my honor.

Team guys nowadays are getting reamed for not maintaining a professional appearance. Our profession is war, and we should look like warriors. We aren't in the profession of looking good, we are in the profession of killing people and destroying things; so while you're standing in front of the mirror polishing your boots, counting your ribbons, and looking good the men will be in the field or in the gym or, God forbid, beating some pinko's ass at the bar... In a brotherhood of warriors, you are only as strong as your weakest man. Well, we are letting weaker men slip through the cracks every day. Soon it is going to bite us in the ass.

There is a distinct difference between the Navy and the Navy SEAL Teams. If a man spent 10 years in the Navy before getting through BUD/S and into the Teams, he would still be a new guy, regardless of his rank, because this is a different community. We have lost sight of what makes us different and special, and we are conforming to the standards of others, and forgetting about those set by our fathers and brothers before us. In fact, as a community, we have completely forgotten... If we accept the fact that most of our leaders believe that form takes precedence over function, then we can all be one family again and we can reward each other with silver stars after deployment even though all we did was sit in the TOC and complain about bad comms. Excuse me for arguing with the idea that the most prudent "go, no-go criteria" are ensuring good comms with people in the TOC who have no control over the actions on; or having a neat, attractive 'PowerPoint' presentation for the mission briefs when really we could have spent that time getting ourselves ready to kill Muslims. Without these two elements (comms and Powerpoint), SEALs simply cannot operate; even if they have 90 people on target full of bullets, grenades, piss, and vinegar.

Who decided that we needed more officers in the teams? Moreover, who decided that we needed more 'operators' in the teams altogether? We don't need either, holy shit! The enlisted men run the teams?!? Bull-fucking-shit; not anymore. The enlisted guys either paint their noses brown and enjoy 20 years of good evals, or keep their blood red and spend their careers fighting a losing battle. They have only two options and if neither of these is viable, goodbye Navy. Some people want to believe that we haven't lowered our standards, but it's so easy to see that we clearly have and continue to do so.

It's alright though, we'll just flood the teams with more bodies and all our prayers will be answered. First, we'll lower the standards at BUD/S, then we'll make it so painfully difficult and time-consuming to take someone's bird away, that it will be nearly impossible. Then, we'll lower the standards of everything else in NSW and instead of 2,000 special operators, we'll have 5,000 operators. Who needs special anyway? The army doesn't like special and unconventional, so let's just throw that crazy shit out the window and paint the green cookie cutter blue and gold and call it ours.

I am my brother's keeper.

Being a family so dedicated to the US military and knowing the great depth of love Aaron had always felt about the SEAL community, this writing was deeply shocking and beyond disturbing to me. As I said, I could hear Aaron's frustration mounting after his return from deployments.

In 2011, shortly before his last deployment Aaron told me this about the enemy. "Dad, they hate us, but they fear us. Lethal, brute force is all they respect."

I knew my son. I knew that no matter what, Aaron had not and would not ever waiver in his determination and in the strength with which he was still willing to fight for our republic. My family could only hope and trust that the changes we were all seeing by the chain of command were as equally dedicated to our son, as our son was to America.

Aaron's testimonies echoed in my head. It was shocking to know that someone so close to me, my own son, who thought and believed so many things identical to my own views, had given me these threads of truth before he died. Aaron, in my view, understood the Afghan culture better than most Americans. I wondered what the American leadership was missing in all of this? Why couldn't our leaders understand the enemy, or even the Afghanis, who our Special Operators were supporting? Why was the American vision blind to the cultural differences, and why were they re-shaping our strong military to be servants of another country?

I remember asking Aaron a question that still haunts me. "Son, how can you do what you do?"

Aaron answered, "Dad, because they [the military] will not let me die."

Clearly though...they did.

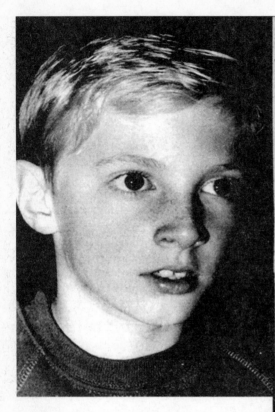

Middle East a concern at Hillcrest

Editor's note: We asked some fourth and fifth grade students at Hillcrest Elementary School the question, "What do you think should be done about the Middle East situation?"

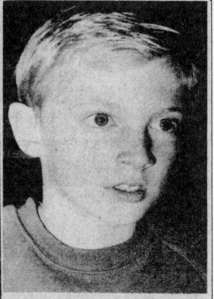

Even in grade school Aaron was keenly aware of world affairs.

Aaron Vaughn: "We shouldn't let them take over a lot of places. Saddam Hussein's intending to take over a lot of places. We should go over there for the sake of young people he's killing with gas."

Through the years, he learned how to handle just about anything you put in front of him.

He never simply "rode" anything. He always had to see just how much he could do with it.

Left:
Teaching his little sister, Ana,
to ride her bike

Below:
You almost never saw Aaron without a
smile on his face.

Aaron's favorite pastime in high school...mudding with his friends.

Enjoying some down time with his grandmothers on the day of Tara's wedding.
"Granny" on the left, "Nanu" on the right.

Since Aaron was the first grandchild on both sides of the family, all the grandparents let
him choose what they'd be called. The names still hold.

Hanging out with Tara & "Daddy Frank."
Frank (Karen's father) passed away August 9, 2001.

Reminiscing with "Papa" at the wedding rehearsal dinner in 2008.

The first time Aaron brought Kimberly home to meet the family.

Enjoying some Florida Keys sunshine with Kimberly, Adam & Tara.

Loving his beautiful bride-to-be.

Aaron, Tara, Kimberly & Ana in DC for the wedding.

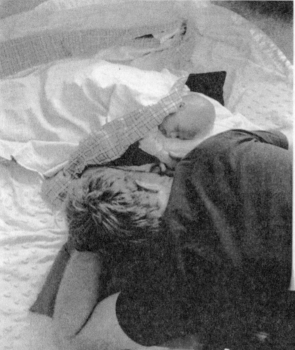

Mesmerized by his tiny son.

Treasuring the last moments with his newborn daughter, days before his final deployment.

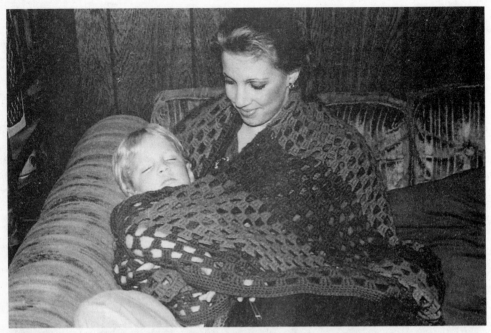

From a baby to a man in what seemed like no time at all.

Seemed like we were always saying goodbye.

Aaron on deployment in Iraq.

BUD/S

Whereabouts unknown.

Having some fun in the mountains of Afghanistan.

Reagan's first visit with Pappy to Aaron's gravesite in Arlington.

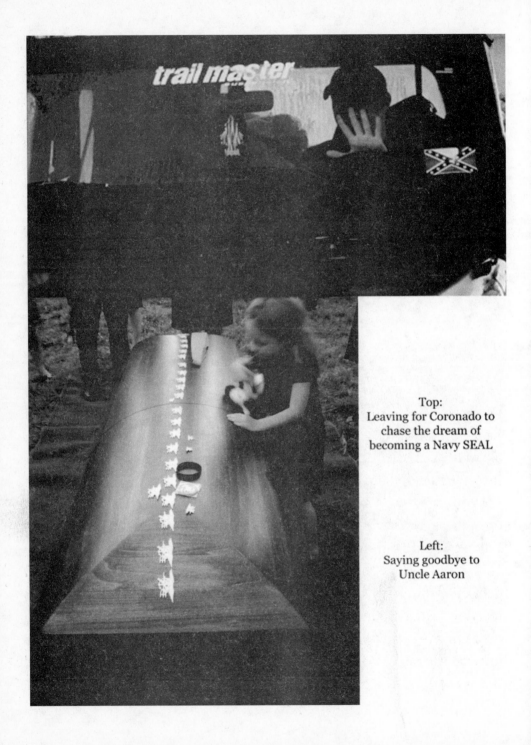

Top:
Leaving for Coronado to
chase the dream of
becoming a Navy SEAL

Left:
Saying goodbye to
Uncle Aaron

6

The Debriefing

Faithful are the wounds of a friend;
but the kisses of an enemy are deceitful.

- Proverbs 27:6 KJV

In October 2011, the parents and spouses of all the fallen heroes of *Extortion 17* were invited to the Naval Amphibious Base Little Creek (NAB) in Virginia Beach, VA. During this meeting, each family was handed a file folder. In it was a printed overview of the military findings as well as a CD that contained extensive documentation of the full investigation, including hundreds of pages of sworn testimony. In full, the CD contained over twelve hundred pages of heavy information. I didn't open these files until three months later, in January 2012, mostly because I didn't want to relive what I thought might be in those pages.

We had all been gathered that October day to hear a lengthy debriefing on what had been uncovered during the investigation. This meeting lasted about five or six hours. Somewhere near the end of the debriefing, we were shown a simulated video of the chopper as it left the forward operating base and made its way toward the hot landing zone. But seconds before the shoot-down, the simulation morphed to the live feed from the Air Weapons Team in the valley. Though the camera's eye was not on the chopper as it approached, we were listening to all of the communication between the various aircraft in the battle zone, right up to those final words none of us will ever forget...

"Fallen angel. We have a fallen angel."

The entire room burst into a simultaneous groan, mixed with soft cries of disbelief and shock, as the cameras finally made their way to the massive explosion of *Extortion 17*.

We had just witnessed the death of our loved ones.

Although we couldn't see a lot of detail in the night-vision video feed, we were told eight of the men were thrown out of the chopper. But we *were* able to make out three different sections of the Chinook that had dropped in random locations—the two rotors, which had been torn away from the fuselage, and of course, the fuselage itself.

Holding a model CH-47D chopper in his hands, Brigadier General Colt then explained that the RPG detonated on contact with a rotor blade on the rear assembly, and immediately compromised the structural integrity of the blade spar box (comprised of a steel rod surrounded by a titanium and fiberglass box). As the spar box distorted due to weapon and flight dynamics, a ten-foot portion of the blade body (behind the spar box and constructed of lightweight fiberglass and honeycomb) was severed from the rotor blade.

The resultant imbalance affected the entire airframe and drive-train subsystem. A sudden and violent ~3.75 Hz oscillation of the entire aft rotor system led to the separation of the aft pylon within two seconds. This caused an immediate loss in lift as well as an unrecoverable clockwise spin. Brigadier General Colt demonstrated as he spoke. The forward rotor system, unable to compensate for the loss of lift and stability throughout the airframe, was stressed beyond design limits and separated in flight. The fuselage subsequently impacted the ground. The entire event, from weapon impact to crash, likely lasted less than five seconds.

As I listened, I prayed the brevity of the event meant Aaron and the others hadn't suffered. But it did nothing to answer any of my lingering questions, especially those surrounding the use of the CH-47D Chinook. I still wanted to know why our special forces were being flown into hot battle zones in these slow, outdated troop transport carriers, rather than the usual MH-47 Chinooks that are designed to get in and out of hotspots quickly.

The statement I'd heard a month earlier at DEVGRU regarding the shortage of proper helos continued grinding in my thoughts: "because we are not engaged in this war." I have great respect for that man because his frank and honest response made me aware of an issue I had not previously understood. Our military leadership was not responding adequately to real and present dangers surrounding the men fighting in the actual theater of battle.

During the debriefing, the additional plausible data being presented painted a clearer picture for me. We were told the reason the team used the older Chinook (CH-47D) instead of the normal and much more capable MH-47 was that the Special Ops teams were on "orders to increase the pressure" on the enemy by accelerating their monthly missions.

Unable to remain silent any longer, I spoke up from the audience. "I understand we only have sixty-one MH-47s."

General Colt affirmed my numbers publicly and later reiterated, "Sir, your numbers are correct."

That meant that although the number of Special Operations missions was drastically stepped up, the increase in missions did not include an upsurge in equipment. This information was also confirmed in General Colt's approximately twelve hundred page investigative report.

In fact, according to some statistics I discovered in the redacted file, in 2009 the average number of Special Op missions per month was fifty-six. In August 2010, the average number had more than tripled to 186 per month. But the worst news was still to come. From August 2010 until July 2011, one month before the shoot-down, the number of Special Op missions had skyrocketed to an astounding 335 per month.[1] In his investigative report, General Colt states, "While the number of strike forces was increased to accommodate the operations, the number of Spec Op Aviation was not." These words were difficult to comprehend.

During a brief lunch break, the families and the military in attendance dispersed into smaller groups and discussions. A high-ranking admiral in attendance spoke with me privately. "Billy, if we have sixty MH-47s, we are only allowed twenty in theater at one time. Twenty must be down for maintenance, and twenty for training."

This was more than disturbing. If there wasn't enough proper equipment to go around, didn't that mean command had made decisions that put my son at unnecessary risk? Were other warriors—other sons—being put under the same kind of risk still?

When the debriefing resumed, I asked, "Why was there no return fire on the enemy once the RPGs had been launched?"

General Colt told the families that they did not return fire because "friendlies" may have been present in the building, and the "Rules of Engagement" (ROE) had prevented them from firing back. What kind of "Rules of Engagement" would keep our men from being able to do their job?

I had no way of knowing how that new awareness would continue to stir my thoughts. At that time, I didn't know enough about these "ROE" to ask any other questions. I just continued listening to what they had to say.

When the presentation was over, I politely asked if I could stay and watch the video again, as did a few other families. General Colt granted permission and invited us to view the video in a private and discreet location downstairs. A lieutenant colonel, who had been part of the investigative team, led the way.

After the second viewing of the video, several of us began to ask more questions. I was having a hard time accepting what General Colt said to us earlier about the ROE, so I asked the lieutenant colonel one more time, "When *Extortion 17* was hit, why was no return fire given?"

The lieutenant colonel repeated General Colt's entire scenario, nearly verbatim, explaining about possible friendlies and stating again, "We didn't return fire because of the Rules of Engagement."

I immediately repeated my question. "You mean to tell me that when *Extortion 17* was hit, no return fire was given because of the Rules of Engagement?"

Karen nudged me, annoyed. "He's already answered you. Stop asking the same question."

But the answer wasn't sitting right with me. It was unimaginable that a chopper with thirty American warriors could have been shot out of the sky and then no return fire followed from the Air Weapons Team above. We had two AH-64 Apache helicopters and an AC-130 gunship overhead, watching the entire scenario unfold. They were first-hand witnesses to the massive explosion where thirty of their brothers lay burning, and yet unable to fire back because of Rules of Engagement? It didn't compute.

Despite Karen's frustration, the lieutenant colonel kindly answered me anyway, "Yes, sir, Mr. Vaughn, it's because of the Rules of

Engagement." That basically concluded the debriefing for Karen and me at the Base.

As I left the room, I reflected on another moment at the debriefing when all of the families were in the amphitheater upstairs. One of the fathers asked why a drone strike wasn't used to take out the target that night rather than sending thirty Americans into battle to capture one man. Three-Star Admiral Robert Harward turned to the families, placed his hand on my wife's knee, and explained that a drone strike wasn't used because "we need to win their hearts and minds."

Apparently drone strikes now damage our efforts to do so? I had to process that one, since our military routinely uses drones to *deter* collateral damage. What were these Rules of Engagement? I began grasping the true, dirty nature of what I was hearing. Admiral Harward, and others who believed as he did, was in the process of attempting to emasculate warriors whose desire was set on defeating a savage enemy.

On that day we were still in a state of disbelief and were unable to respond to a lot of this new evidence. I couldn't fully absorb what I was hearing. As a result of these "rules," American forces experienced the single largest one-day loss of life in their ten years of war against terror. This crash also represented the single largest loss of life in the history of Naval Special Warfare.

With every day, the facts were becoming more and more unsettling.

After Karen and I had some time to absorb the gravity of this debriefing, we became angry and asked each other this question repeatedly: "When and why did winning hearts and minds become a priority over the shed blood of our warriors?"

It is one thing when a warrior freely offers his life in military service to his country. It is quite another for a country to sacrifice that warrior on a fool's errand while trying to appease people who have long proven they couldn't be placated. I had no idea our government policy had changed so drastically. However, something was starting to become very clear: weak-willed "winning hearts and minds" ideology had taken priority over keeping my son, the men on that chopper, our military, and even our nation, secure.

One of the realities you face as a parent of a SEAL is that your son could die. If my son and the others had gone into battle that night on proper equipment, with guns blazing, and had still been shot out of the sky, I would not be writing this book. I would simply be dealing with grief over the loss of my son.

Instead, I had to stomach that this "new" way of waging war had killed my boy, and who knows how many others. Our Special Ops warriors were on orders from above to "relentlessly pursue the enemy," but were required to do so without the proper equipment and with both hands tied behind their backs due to restrictive ROE.

I know my son. Aaron Vaughn did not become a Navy SEAL to "win the hearts and minds" of anyone. He became a SEAL to crush enemies of the nation he loved so much. But don't be mistaken by thinking a warrior with that kind of determination and valor doesn't have an equal measure of compassion and mercy.

I will never forget one story Aaron told about storming a house. As the SEALs cleared the building, their eyes landed on a woman standing among the men of that particular terror cell. The team spared her, although she was likely as complicit in the terror ring as any man in the house. When moving from room to room, Aaron noticed a blanket on the floor. Something underneath it moved. With the tip of his gun he lifted the corner and discovered a baby, abandoned by the woman who had fled the building. With full knowledge that the baby could have been strapped with a bomb, one of the men—disregarding his own safety—picked the child up, cradled it, and then called the woman back to the house where he placed the baby safely in her arms.

By the end of October 2011, I began to call members of our US Congress. Each time I'd say, "My name is Billy Vaughn. I'm the father of Aaron Vaughn, member of SEAL Team VI who was killed two months ago in the shoot-down of *Extortion 17* in Afghanistan. I would like to speak to Congressman/Senator _____ regarding a couple of issues about what happened in the crash. Here is my phone number. He can call me at his earliest convenience."

I called Speaker John Boehner's office. No response.

I called Senator Harry Reid. No response.

Senator Carl Levin's staff actually told me, "The Senator does *not* have time to speak with you." I continued calling his office only because Senator Levin served as Chairman of the Senate Armed Services Committee, the committee responsible for appropriations of proper military equipment. After my third or fourth very polite request, I was told to stop harassing him.

While making all of these calls, the only time I expressed any frustration was when I was speaking with a member of Senator Marco Rubio's staff. I had called his office two days in a row. The first day I explained to his receptionist that Senator Rubio had sent a representative to Aaron's memorial in Florida, expressing his personal regret that he couldn't be there himself. I also explained that Senator Rubio had sent word to us: "If you need anything, please call my office." I asked her to please leave a message that I did, in fact, need the Senator's help.

I called on the second day, a Friday, and asked if Senator Rubio received my message. If the answer had been "yes," I simply planned to thank her and wait patiently for his call. Instead the receptionist snapped back sharply, "Sir, Senator Rubio is *not* going to call you over the weekend."

I told her I didn't expect to receive a call over the weekend. I politely recounted the details of our conversation the day before and repeated my phone number. I had learned enough to know that I needed to ask her to confirm she had recorded my number correctly, to make sure the Senator could reach me when he received the message.

She was unable to repeat the phone number back to me.

I asked, "You didn't even write it down, did you?"

The receptionist neither admitted nor denied, and simply asked me for my number again. Not surprisingly, I didn't hear from Senator Rubio or anyone from his office during that phase of my investigation. More than one year later, however, after his office was notified that I had publicly commented on my interaction with his staff, they quickly contacted me and were very apologetic.

The only responses I received from my phone calls in that month were from three Congressmen: Representative Stephen Fincher, Representative Allen West, and my representative, Thomas Rooney. They all asked if they could assist my family and me with additional answers.

On our behalf, Representative Rooney requested and was given a Top Secret meeting with high-level military officials to discuss details of the shoot-down of *Extortion 17*. A year-and-a-half later, I learned another congressman from Florida, Representative and Colonel Allen West, was also present at this classified meeting. At the conclusion of the hearing, I received this follow-up letter
from Congressman Rooney, about three days before Christmas in 2011.

THOMAS J. ROONEY
16TH DISTRICT, FLORIDA

12 DEC 11

U.S. HOUSE OF REPRESENTATIVES

MR VAUGN —

At your request and per our conversation I had a high level top secret hearing with members of the military in our oversight committee. Also in attendance was our Chairman from Virginia Rob Wittman and staff. We went through the entire episode which led to the crash of the CH-47 in Wardak which killed your son. Again, I can't tell you how sorry I am and can't imagine the pain your family has to endure. The questions we talked about on the phone made matters worse which is why I requested the meeting. I believe you said you had a similar briefing. Although I am not completely satisfied with some of the decisions, I left the meeting feeling at least the Rules of Engagement did not inhibit the mission. As a Judge Advocate, I have been most critical of how we wage war today. That being said I can tell you the house the RPGs were fired out of whas not positively identifiable by the

Apache helicopters in the area. They only had a peripheral view of the location they originated from. The CH-47 went into an immediate spin upon being hit. It could therefore not have returned fire. The men who shot the RPGs were killed within 48 hours of the crash thanks to cell phone intel. The military also assured me Blackhawks were available but were not used because the Cmdr wanted mass forces right away. That is the biggest area of dispute. It was a judgement call by him and obviously the wrong one. We were assured the pilots had over 100 hrs of combat experience and over 500 hrs flying on top of that. The Taliban was ready for us that day. We got into a grove of doing things the same way on these missions and underestimated the enemy. I am sorry none of this can bring you comfort. I have 3 sons and cannot imagine what you are going through. I will keep you in my prayers. keep the faith.

FL 16

We were approaching our first Christmas without Aaron, which was tough, and I wasn't prepared for what Rooney had written: "I left the meeting feeling at least the Rules of Engagement didn't inhibit the mission."

What?

I needed time to think about my reaction. It was definitely a one-way communication. I didn't have an opportunity to respond to him immediately as I would have if this information had been discussed by phone.

I let the letter sit for about two weeks, and by then my list of questions had only expanded. Who were these people who gave the Top Secret hearing and why would someone lie about the Rules of Engagement and the reason for the lack of return fire? Remember, I had been told three times at Little Creek Base that because of the Rules of Engagement, our men in the military could not take out the enemy after the chopper had been shot down.

Things weren't adding up. What was Congressman Rooney talking about when he was referring to "how we wage war today"? With which "decisions" was he "not completely satisfied"?

I needed further discussion with the investigative team who had briefed the families. So in early January 2012, I spoke with the lieutenant colonel who had taken us downstairs for the additional viewing of the crash footage back in October.

"Can you repeat what you told us at the debriefing about our inability to return fire after the chopper had been shot down?" I asked him. The lieutenant colonel went into more detail than before. He said, "One AH-64 saw it [the RPG shot] out of their peripheral, the other AH-64 saw where the RPGs came from. The shots were fired from a tower over a building, and the pilots and aircrew could not tell if there were friendlies in the building below the tower."

I wasn't ready to reveal to the lieutenant colonel that I was aware people were lying about the chopper crash. I had to know more before I could react fairly and figure out who was being truthful and who was not. So that was the end of our conversation.

The fact that the shots were fired from a tower on top of a building was new information to me. Did that mean the "hostiles"—who were overtly attacking our men—were visible in the tower? And why was I just learning this five months after Aaron's death?

Immediately after that, I called Admiral Sean Pybus, who was present with the families on the day of the debriefing. Admiral Pybus had also graciously flown to and spoken at Aaron's first memorial service in West Tennessee just a week after we'd been notified of his death. I didn't disclose to him at the time that I had spoken with the lieutenant colonel, but I did reveal that I received a letter from Congressman Rooney. I explained that somebody from the military at a Top Secret hearing in Washington, D.C. lied, saying they didn't know where the shots came from.

"Why would they say that?" I asked.

Admiral Pybus said he didn't know.

"We know where the shots were fired from, don't we? We were told on that day in the debriefing that RPGs were fired from the building and no return fire was given because of the ROE, right?"

The admiral replied, "Billy, you heard the same thing I heard."

Determined to no longer rely on others for the answers I needed, I dug out the redacted files we received at Little Creek. I could *never* have imagined what I was about to learn.

7

Disturbing Discoveries

*Whatever you have said in the dark will be
heard in the light, and what you have
whispered behind closed doors will be
shouted from the housetops for all to hear!*

- Luke 12:3 NLT

As I placed the CD from the debriefing into the computer for the very first time, I felt a nauseating sense of dread. I had no concept of what I was about to unearth, or how painful the process would be. However, I understood that if Karen and I were to know the full truth of what happened on that dark night in history, it would be up to us to uncover it. We labored through all the minute-by-minute investigation results, the official reports, and the testimony of the individuals who witnessed the entire event.

To say the least, this was gut-wrenching. Each PDF, Word document, PowerPoint, and spreadsheet we opened painted a more complete picture of Aaron's death—the last few seconds of his life. This was the who, what, when, where, and how. We read about the enemy forces in the area, the planning—which took place hours ahead of the shoot-down—the loading up of the chopper, the flight to the landing zone, and the location and activity of the Taliban members who fired the RPGs.

But none of that prepared us for what came next—the moment of impact—the heart wrenching words of the pilots who watched—the explosions, and then *every* detail of what happened in the aftermath and investigation.

We studied maps of the Tangi River Valley and viewed all the images of the chopper as it laid on the ground in pieces. We wanted to know what Aaron knew. What he saw. We wondered if he had time to think. Did he know what was happening to him? As tormenting as it was, however, the more deeply I read the materials and viewed the images, the more determined I became to finish this work.

I am an American who loves this republic.

I had to know what was going on with our military.

Within hours of opening the redacted files—large sections removed completely—my sadness had morphed into rage. I was shocked the military had placed this much damning information in our laps and sickened I had come so close to never looking at it. Remember, had a high-ranking military official not lied to my congressman, I more than likely would never have placed the CD in my computer.

By the time I had read through the entire document, I came to the appalling realization that the mightiest military in the world is being ripped asunder by a regime in Washington, D.C., putrefied with political correctness, moral depravity, and utter corruption.

The documentation I am about to share is no longer classified. This information was given, not only to us, but also to all the parents and/or spouses who attended the debriefing. I will share the facts as I found them.

The facts are enough.

The first shocking discovery we made was finding out the Afghan government is involved in the entire Special Ops mission planning process. In the redacted file, r_EX01, pages 6-7, we read the following: (Note: GIRoA is an acronym for Government of the Islamic Republic of Afghanistan)

SECRET//NOFORN

Likewise you see on the left there the OCG. We made some real money with the OCG; they are the Operational Coordination Group and they assist us with the planning, and the vetting, and de-confliction of our operation. Likewise once we are done executing the operation they are able to send the results report, the result of the operations up through their various administrates. They are made up of the ANA, Afghan National Army, the National Director for Security, as well as the National Police Force. They are here on site. They are here on site, but we also have them down at the regional level in RC-South and in September we are going to stand up region site up in RC-North.

IO-DEP: So they have visibility on every operation?

⬛)ı4a, ()ı⬛: Every operation.

IO-DEP: So they knew about the operations.

⬛)ı4a, ()ı⬛: Oh yea.

IO-DEP: And they were briefed on it.

⬛)ı4a, ()ı⬛: Absolutely. And (b)(3), (b)(6) – is there, are they going to visit the EOCG as well.

JSOAC CDR: Umm not planned, but we can start the process.

⬛)ı4a, ()ı⬛: Yea, I would definitely recommend that.

IO-DEP: So they have the ability, do they have approval authority on that, to cancel an operation?

~~SECRET//NOFORN~~

~~SECRET//NOFORN~~

⬛)ı4a, ()ı⬛: Technically they do, they don't exercise it, but technically they do have authority.

IO-DEP: So they either task or approve the operation.

⬛)ı4a, ()ı⬛: Yep. ▓▓▓▓▓▓▓▓▓▓▓▓▓▓▓

Also see r_EX01, page 9:

116

██████████████████████████████████████ And then a big
change in 2009 and 2010 as we move towards sovereignty, every
operation is coordinated through GIRoA. [The] enduring Task
Force footprint – again it will ██ ██ ██tal strike forces with
associated ISR. ████████████████████████████

Yes, every operation is coordinated through the Government of the Islamic Republic of Afghanistan—every operation.

r_EX01, page 59:

BG Colt: Well, it does indirectly; right? Because every
mission including LEFTY GROVE is vetted through these guys;
true?

JSOTF J3: ████████████ So the Operational Coordination
Group, it was formed over two years ago when we said we needed
to have really better legitimacy in the eyes of GIRoA in order
to maintain our freedom of maneuver. So, these guys are high
level officials from Ministry of Defense, Ministry of Interior,
and the National Directorate of Security. There are ██(b)(1)1.4a, (b)(1)1.4c
teams right now. They go on 24 hour shifts and they sit in a
JOC right next to ours; and you can go visit it really anytime

r_EX01, page 60: Speaking still about the Afghani Operational Coordination Group:

```
they watch all our ISR, they'll see our JOC blogs, they will

hear the radio calls.  Really the only thing we keep from them,

obviously, is the TS level how we got to the target piece of

it.  They are briefed on all the targets prior to execution

and, you know, technically speaking if they would come to us

and say, "I don't want you to execute this mission," we

wouldn't do it.  Not because they have—it's because internally

we have kind of given them that say.  ████████████████████
```

We are placing our Special Operators under the watch care of Afghanis. Any American with common sense knows by now that many of our so-called Afghan allies cannot be trusted. By allowing the OCG veto power in mission planning, you *could* say our Special Operators are being forced to work under the authority of the Afghan Government rather than the nation to which they pledged their lives. While reading these files, I got the impression that President Obama had generously loaned the Navy SEALs to the Afghan government, unbeknownst to the American people.

In May 2013, several family members of the fallen men of *Extortion 17* held a national press conference, asking Congress to open a special investigation into the shoot-down. Shortly afterward, a former military intelligence operator contacted Karen and me. Later that afternoon the three of us sat down for a private meeting where we learned that his duties, during his last deployment, included vetting the Afghanis who work alongside America's Special Operators. He told us about the difficulties his team faced while trying to vet these men. According to him, the vetting process "is extremely difficult since it never really ends, due to shifting loyalties among the Afghani Commandos."

We then inquired about the OCG. His immediate reply was: "Our Intel men fear this group more than any other...specifically they fear Pakistani infiltration." He went on to explain that due to a special agreement between Afghan President Hamid Karzai and the Obama Administration, the members of this elite organization were above our vetting process. And the shocking news didn't stop there. He further explained that this group is allowed to function with absolutely no US oversight.

According to the records we've been given, there is no evidence any members of the OCG were ever questioned during the military investigation of the shoot-down.

The OCG is off limits.

My son's words haunted me. "Dad, they are only loyal to the highest bidder."

The second discovery we made was learning that the words coming from the White House regarding the identity of our nation's enemies, conflicted with those coming from the men and women in the field of battle.

During an interview with *Newsweek* in December 2011—four months after the Taliban shot our warriors from the sky—Vice-President Joe Biden made the following statement, "Look, the Taliban per se is not our enemy. That's critical."[1] Later that week, Press Secretary Jay Carney publicly stood by Joe Biden's ludicrous statement.

The testimony of military leaders in Afghanistan describes quite a contrasting picture.

r_EX01, page 12: (Describing the al Qaeda network)

The other thing is they are very much invested in the
Taliban fight. Ok, if the Taliban wins at the end of the day
over here in Afghanistan, then that is a win for Al-Qaeda. So
they are "all in" as far as the Taliban is concerned. When Al-
Qaeda is operating in Afghanistan they are operating under that
Taliban hat. ████████████████████████████████████

r_EX01, page 13:

When you are in Afghanistan, you are fighting the Taliban
- that is the bottom line. Mullah Mohammad Omar is the leader;

r_EX01, page 14:

████████████████████████████████████ We do see some
Talban specific up in there, but again anywhere you are
fighting in Afghanistan you are fighting Taliban. ███████████

Speaking of Mullah Mohammed Omar...On August 16, 2012, The
Long War Journal blog reported the following:

In this year's Eid al Fitr message to the Afghan
people, Taliban supremo Mullah Omar addressed the issues of the green-on-blue attacks (Afghan forces attacking
ISAF troops) and the infiltration of the Afghan security
forces. Mullah Omar, claims that the Taliban "cleverly infiltrated in the ranks of the enemy according to the plan giv-

en to them last year." He urges government officials and security personnel to defect and join the Taliban, as it is their religious duty to do so, and then warns that "the day is not far away that the invading enemy will flee Afghanistan." He also notes that the Taliban have created the "Call and Guidance, Luring and Integration" department, "with branches...now operational all over the country," to encourage defections.[1]

In mid-2012, a high-ranking admiral explained to me, "There has been no real progress in Afghanistan for months now." After reading the information above, is there *any* question left as to why? Good men and women are dying, and the question must be answered. Why can't our leaders recognize *their own failed strategy?*

In r_EX01, page 1 (to establish date of interview) and pages 14-15, additional confirmation is provided that indicates our leaders are completely out of touch with issues pertaining to US national security:

~~SECRET//NOFORN~~

The interview occurred on 15 August 2011 at Bagram AB.

Finally, the Haqqani network. The Haqqani network is led by Siraj Haqqani and he's got his brother, Badruddin Haqqani, they are running it from the Miram Shah sanctuary. Miram Shah is about 22 kilometers across the border. They are interested in P2K [Paktika, Paktya and Khowst provinces], they have family ties [and] tribal ties in that area. ████████████████

SECRET//NOFORN

SECRET//NOFORN

████████████████ No external aspirations – they want to be the king of the roost right in this area now and in the future. [They have a] tremendous amount of ability to push forces cross the board. We consider them the most lethal, resolute, and resilient of the insurgent element[s] we are fighting today. They have the ability to push forces across, conduct attacks – they will actually see to the attacks themselves. Haqqani routinely comes up in comms during the attacks, getting SITREPS from the elements he has conducting the attack.

Noting the date on the redacted file above "15 August 2011," you'll see that our then Secretary of State, Hillary Clinton, apparently had not received the memo on the Haqqani Network. On August 31, *2012*, more than a year after our military intel described that network as "the most lethal, most resolute, and resilient of the insurgent element[s] we are *fighting* today" [*Italics mine*], the Huffington Post reported the following: "US Secretary of State Hillary Rodham Clinton said Friday she will meet next week's deadline to report to Congress on whether the Haqqani network should be designated as a terrorist organization."[2]

On September 7, 2012, ABC News reported: "Secretary of State Hillary Clinton said today she plans to officially name the Haqqani network, a violent Taliban-affiliated militant group based in Pakistan, as a terrorist organization."[3]

What a joke.

Once again, we witness a deadly failure by our government to acknowledge in a timely fashion the enemies of our fighting men and women. All the while, our warriors *must* address their enemies, on a daily basis, in life and death situations, without the benefit of national leaders who understand or acknowledge them.

As troubling as these revelations were, some of the most puzzling questions began while reading through the events of the night, as witnessed by members of the Air Weapons Team circling above the ongoing engagement.

Remember, the Rangers were sent in on the initial mission to capture Qari Tahir. Their helo dropped them south of the village, which they were to engage. As they advanced toward that village, squirters departed the east and west rear quadrants and headed north up the Tangi River Valley.

Following is a description of what the AC-130 Gunship crew witnessed while keeping eyes on the squirters leaving the eastern rear quadrant. Also remember, as you read the transcript below, this operation took place in the dead of night, which makes the "tactical movement" north toward the insertion point—the landing zone—of the IRF (Immediate Reaction Force – the Navy SEALs) much more suspicious.

r_EX40, pages 10-11:

TELEVISION SENSOR OPERATOR: Before they gained access to that piece of terrain up there, we maintained chain of custody the

~~SECRET~~

~~SECRET~~

entire time while tracking them. They were stopping, they were moving tactically in the tree line, stopping at compounds, picking up individuals and by the time they got to this piece of terrain they had already had eight individuals total at that time, so they had picked up six pax along the way.

IO-DEP: Okay.

TELEVISION SENSOR OPERATOR: And they were all moving tactically, running, at that time.

r_ENCL B, page 21:

The enemy killed-in-action (EKIA) near the original target area (by the AWT and 1/B assault force) were armed with RPGs and AK-47s, and were wearing chest racks filled with grenades and AK-47 magazines, indicating that they were preparing to respond to coalition operations. Additionally, the assault force discovered two VHF handheld radios on the bodies of the EKIA which could be used for command and control and as part of an active early warning network reporting on coalition forces in the Tangi Valley. In addition to the EKIA, eight or nine other individuals – suspected Taliban fighters, included the two who had departed the target area towards the northwest – gathered near the planned insertion point of the IRF.

These testimonies indicate that the Apache pilots were keeping eyes on the heavily armed squirters leaving the *western* rear quadrant. Note especially the last line, "gathered near the planned insertion point of the IRF." (Immediate Reaction Force – the Navy SEALs) The big question here is: how did the enemy know where the IRF insertion point would be?

But the largest concern had yet to be uncovered. In r_EX 01, page 118, we learned the seven Afghan Commandos who died on the chopper were not the men listed on the flight manifest.

> **IO-DEP:** Was there a manifest for that aircraft back at the --
>
> **JSOTF J3:** Yes, sir. And I'm sure you know by now the manifest was accurate with the exception of the (b)(1)1.4a, (b)(1) personnel that were on. So the [(b)(1)1.4a, (b)(1)1.4c] personnel, they were the incorrect -- all seven names were incorrect. And I cannot talk to the back story of why, but --

Upon discovery of this alarming information, I immediately yelled to Karen, "You need to see this!" We spent a great deal of time discussing the possible reasons for this incorrect manifest. We finally settled between ourselves that most likely this was done to protect the identities of the Afghanis on board, thus protecting their loved ones. At this stage, we were still determined to believe our government was not hiding or covering anything up.

We were naïve.

Almost one year later, four-star Admiral William McRaven visited our home. During that meeting we would learn that this piece of information would surge our suspicions forward remarkably.

I made a nonchalant statement about the manifest being incorrect in regard to the names of the seven Afghanis on board: "I guess it wasn't a big deal, right? Because that was all that was said about it and it was then just passed over."

An advisor present with the admiral that day responded with something to the effect of, "It was a very big deal, Mr. Vaughn. That should never have happened. In fact, all of the Afghan families who had previously been notified of their loved ones' death had to be re-notified that they were, in fact, alive. What actually happened was, at the last minute, the *commander* wanted to swap out those listed for the seven Afghanis who were actually on the chopper."

A few hours after the admiral and advisor had left our home, two very important questions surfaced in my mind:

What *commander*? And *why*?

I pondered that thought for the next few days before deciding how, exactly, I should proceed. Finally, I called my contact at SOCOM (Special Operations Command), who had participated in the investigation. This was the same lieutenant colonel who took the families downstairs after the debriefing to review the films in a private setting.

After rehearsing the conversation that had taken place at our home regarding the last-minute swap, I posed the question, "Can you tell me who that commander was?"

He hesitated momentarily then spoke with a quiet, but clearly perplexed tone, "Mr. Vaughn, we weren't told about that [the last minute swap, which left the manifest incorrect]. I find that very puzzling since the Afghanis who should have been on that chopper would have been men your son and his team had been training and had worked with for some time." My mind struggled for understanding. What *possible* explanation could there be for keeping this critical information from the investigative team?

Once again, the more we learned, the more questions we had.

The Tangi River Valley was and is still extremely dangerous. According to military records (r_EX86, page 3) we cleared that valley on seven prior occasions in the past three years alone. Seven. What allowed the "hostiles" to return? Wouldn't that be like taking Normandy beach, allowing the Germans to come back, and then taking it again—seven times?

See below, in an excerpt from r_ENCL B, page 7, the threat assessment of the Tangi River Valley on the night of the fatal shoot-down:

(a) (S//REL USA, ISAF, NATO) The Tangi Valley was assessed as a moderate to high threat to coalition forces based on reported enemy activities, historical surface-to-air fire reports by coalition forces aircraft, and the lack of coalition forces presence in the valley.[41] On 5 August 2011, TF and 10th Combat Aviation Brigade (10th CAB) intelligence analysts assessed the threat in the valley as high risk due to: historical enemy activities including RPG and small arms fire, an assessed early warning network, the lack of a coalition force presence in the valley, the significance of the target (Qari Tahir), and the corresponding actions the Tangi Valley Taliban would likely take to prevent his capture.[42]

In the previous two years, our Special Ops missions had been ramped up to such an extent that conventional choppers and crews, rather than Special Forces Aviation, were being utilized routinely in an effort to keep up with a new strategy called, "the relentless pursuit of the enemy." Notice r_ENCL B, page 23 below: (SOF indicates Special Operations Forces)

g. (S//REL, USA) Finding #7. operational tempo exceeds the capacity of organic SOF aviation. ████████████████████

It's worth repeating because it's difficult to read, "operational tempo exceeds the capacity of organic SOF aviation." This indicates that there is not enough SOF aviation for our Special Operations Forces.

r_ENCL B, page 8 addresses the inappropriate and dangerous use of the CH-47D (Cargo-Helicopter, Delta Model) in this relentless pursuit:

(b) (S//REL USA, ISAF, NATO) *Risk and GPF Aviation Support.* The TF ▓(b)(1)1.4a, (b)(1)1.4c Commander was responsible for the initial risk assessment for the CH-47Ds and AH-64Ds in direct support of ▓(b)(1)1.4a, (b)(1) He assessed all missions with ▓(b)(1)1.4a, (b) as high risk based on the compressed planning timeline required to support their high pace of operations.[56] His TF ▓(b)(1)1.4a, (b)(1)1.4c helicopters had conducted ▓(b)(1)1.4a, (b) missions in support of ▓(b)(1)1.4a, (b) over the previous 10 months, all of which were assessed as high risk for CH-47D aircrews.[57] ▓

r_EX 48, page 46 drives the nail a bit deeper:

TF▓(b)(1)1.4a, (b)(1) CDR: I understand the Delta Model is the least

capable model compared to, like, the Golf Model.

I need to take a moment here to explain something. Up until the investigation of this horrific shoot-down, Special Operators and conventional aircrews did not train together in the States. They were thrown into battle with each other, meeting for the very first time in theater.

As a recommendation after the crash, General Colt stated that General Purpose Forces (GPF) should be training with the Special Operations Forces (SOF) *before* they meet in theater.

But even in light of the fact that a very high-risk mission was underway using an ill-equipped CH-47D—a huge, floating "school bus" if you will—the pilots had no escorting choppers leading the way to that HLZ (Hot Landing Zone). Apparently we didn't have enough equipment available to offer proper protection. So on that mission, standard operating procedures were violated.

r_EX 48, page 22 address the standard procedure for utilizing the CH-47D:

TF(b)(1)1.4a, (b)(1) CDR: Yeah. They can't even take off, off the FOB here without an escort at night. ████████████████████

In addition, the AC-130 gun crew made the following observation regarding their lack of comfort with this operation in testimony recorded in r_EX 40, pages 36-37:

████████████ So, it was kind of not normal operations for us to lock both of our sensors down at two different locations because it's kind of asking for us to be kind of vulnerable, I guess. We put our teams in a vulnerable spot, so with that, I mean, that was kind of hard for us to swallow because we couldn't have eyes-on and that's why our pilot had to talk everybody on and

SECRET
SECRET

our visual sensors had to let everybody know what was going on because we were basically south of what was going on from everything else. Our eyes were somewhere else, so that's why our hands were tied as far as that goes.

IO-DEP: Okay. Thank you.

AIRCRAFT COMMANDER: The plan that we had was for AWT to escort the Helos in and they pointed out that a point where we were tracking a 380B so we had clearly coordinated with them, "this is what we are looking at" and "this is where we think the threat is" and they've got primary task, this group of Helos. That was the contract going in. It was a little non-standard, but, in our opinion, was talking about in the crew, it seemed just rushed and we were trying to figure out why exactly it was being so rushed for those eight individuals.

IO-EP: Okay.

NAVIGATOR: I think on station, at this time, we had [(b)(3), (b)(6)] and then [(b)(3), (b)(6)] and then ourselves, and I think at this point Draco was gone because this was after 2100.

It is worth noting here that commanders in theater on that fateful night later stated, in r_EX 88, page 4, that in hundreds of missions, they'd *never* done one like this.

███████████we have had cases were we have put the battle spaces owner in on the ground using for SSE or KLEs after the event. That is a version of a sequel, but like this where we have gone in and put an IRF or reaction force of some sort on there, I can't think of one off the top of my head. It might be one out there, I just don't remember, 100s but I can't recall one and I'm not sure if you can either the way this one happened.

Adding insult to injury for this highly unusual troop insertion, there appeared to be quite a bit of confusion throughout the already active battle space. No one had been assigned to put eyes on the landing zone. See r_EX 53, page 62:

SME GFN1: At any time when you came and checked in and got the handover from ☐(b)(3),(b)(6)☐ or ☐(b)(3),(b)(6)☐ on the squirters, did they talk about the condition of the LZ or the area surrounding it at all?

PB65FS: Honestly, sir, I don't think anybody had really looked at the LZ. I mean, at any time if we would have found these squirters, or they would have found weapons, we were -- the way I was understanding it, we were going to be clear to engage due to the fact that they had weapons, but we had to PID them first.

So we hadn't started looking at the LZ yet, just due to there was so much more of a threat to the east with the squirters. I would say that on the three-minute call is when Gun 2 started -- you see a system on the tape -- start looking at the LZ, giving an LZ brief op. I would say that was the first time that we really had eyes on the LZ.

We quickly understood that even though thirty Americans were being transported into a three-and-a-half-hour battle, in a sixties-era helicopter, in a hostile valley—no one had been assigned to look at the landing zone.

Remember the two individuals the entire QRF was spun up to capture? r_EX 83, page 37 provides evidence that on August 6, 2011, the price of our "hearts and minds" campaign became another thirty American lives.

AIRCRAFT COMMANDER: To the 'X' -- you know, when the original Op was to an off-set essentially, to hike in on foot to the objective for the element of surprise and you're bringing in a Helo, essentially an X to these squirters that we we're tracking after we'd been there for three hours. I think that's what we're getting at.

NAVIGATOR: I think also, too, going back, the original engagement with the AWT, they had PID all eight of those individuals hostile. We tracked two off, and the fact that we were tracking them the entire way -- two clicks. There were several opportunities where we could have engaged with 40MM ensuring 0 CDE (Collateral Damage Estimate) on any buildings. The opportunity was definitely there for us to engage those two guys or even provide containment fires to try to slow their movement. I think that that was also probably [inaudible] --

IO: Did you ask to engage them?

NAVIGATOR: Yes, sir.

IO: And it was denied by 2-3; right?

NAVIGATOR: Yes, sir.

AIRCRAFT COMMANDER: I think he spoke with [redacted], the Ground Force Commander and he said, "No. No-go. Just maintain eyes-on."

In later testimony (r_EX 40, pages 6-7), the aircraft commander once again reiterated that he had asked permission to kill the two heavily armed "squirters" positioning themselves near the landing zone of *Extortion 17*:

AIRCRAFT COMMANDER: Really quick an important point I think at this juncture is), we had requested to engage those two individuals and we were denied----

IO: By the JTAC?

IE: By the JTAC, by [(b)(3), (b)(6)] I think you coordinated with his [(b)(3), (b)(6)] ground force commander they had gotten denied. The original engagement the AWT's was looking at conducting on those pax was a hell fire engagement; they elected to go to the

~~SECRET~~

~~SECRET~~

30 millimeter due to CDE constraints. We pushed 40 millimeter engagements is a 0 CDE (CDE Collateral Damage Estimate) weapon and we were denied that-- we were just requested to maintain track on those two squirters that were moving west.

I had to think about that for a second. The first thing that came to me was that our military men wanted to prevent something. Zero collateral damage means innocent people *won't* get shot. The commander is stating that there was "zero" estimate of innocent people getting shot if the squirters were pursued, yet the commander clearly states they were denied the ability to shoot the "hostiles," also known as the squirters.

By whose logic would the aircrew not be allowed to take out terrorists that had just been engaged in gunfire with the ground crew?

But this is where the report gets muddy. The commander who was present at the event says that the squirters are hostile, no question. General Colt, on page twelve of the official RoI, details all the gunfire on the ground and discusses the activity of the *"assessed enemy personnel."* But somehow a decision was made to send soldiers rather than utilizing an air strike in order to "determine whether the group was armed?"

"The TF [redacted] commander considered his options, including a strike by AC-130 or the AWT, but was unable to determine whether the group was armed and therefore could not authorize the strike."[4]

This seemed very strange to me, and begged another question. What does this commander fear? Is there a true fear of consequences should he utilize lethal force? How far does he have to go to "prove" lethal force was necessary?

Unable to conceive a way this story could get any worse, we were once again stunned. Notice what it says in r_EX83, page 35:

▇▇▇▇▇▇▇▇▇▇▇▇▇▇▇▇I'm not sure, it just appeared to us the whole plan for getting into this area was rushed, I guess. I don't know if that's the case, but that's kind of one thing that I thought might have been done a little bit better.

NAVIGATOR: One of the other things that we did talk about -- kind of what you're hitting on, sir, is about the fact that, you know, for three hours we had been burning holes in the sky. You've got AWT flying around, so there's a lot of noise going on and basically, this entire valley knows that there's something happening in this area. So, to do an infil on the X or Y, you know, having that element of surprise in the beginning of an operation is good, but by the time we've been there for three hours, and the party's up, bringing in another air craft like that, you know, may not be the most tactically sound decision.

r_EX 83, page 36:

▇▇▇▇▇▇▇▇▇▇▇▇▇▇▇▇So, there were still two individuals at that point out there that they knew were hostile, still had weapons and still had the intent of engaging the friendlies at that point, from what we saw in the back because they had already took contact from them. Not only that, but they engaged the individuals in the beginning, you know, and they are all PID'd with weapons. It's just didn't feel comfortable to us to bring another helo in, especially not having a ground team down there securing an LZ for them.

The most shocking news had not yet been uncovered. With clear and present danger in full view, and men scrambling to keep eyes on the terrorists staging themselves near the landing zone, no pre-assault fire was offered.

Aaron had told me that there was only one time a SEAL was vulnerable—during chopper transport and landing, because that's the only time they weren't in control of their situation. I assumed it was standard procedure to provide escorts with pre-assault fire while landing in a hot zone. r_EX53, page 14-15 nearly finished me:

```
PB65FS:  We have to take the 47s in on all the LZs.  So
that's a big reason why we are with [ (b)(3), (b)(6) ] every time.
We are not cleared for pre-assault fires or anything like
```

SECRET

SECRET

```
that.
```

In r_EX53, page 70, the Task Force Commander and a Ground Force Subject Matter Expert are discussing the ROEs and the use of pre-assault fire. Here is the exchange:

TF KH CDR: And to get back to your question about pre-assault fires, the ROE and tactical directorate are pretty specific about what we can and can't do.

Ground Force SME: From my experience, pre-assault fires are next to impossible. Containment fires, I mean, you guys do it all the time. I'm just wondering if there was any talk about that because, I mean, sometimes just to draw attention. I just wanted to clarify. Thank you.

Yes, sir, "Sometimes just to draw attention."

I think that's the least these great American warriors deserved that night.

But the final blow came when we read, first hand, that the Air Weapons Team flying above, gave clear testimony to the fact that they'd seen the point of origin of the launched RPGs that night. We were once again reminded and infuriated that we'd been lied to about the lack of return fire on the enemies who shot our warriors from the sky.

r_EX 40, page 40:

████ You could see the explosion very clearly and you could see the point of origin where the RPG came through. So, at that point, there's no doubt in my mind exactly where it came from and the Helo is on the deck.

r_EX40, page 34:

SECRET

█████████████ On the northeast side of this building there
was a turret, almost like a man-made defensive fighting position
on top of a building that was elevated about 20 to 30 feet. It
definitely had about a three or four foot wall in front, rounded
off, had good line of sight, good 360 coverage for that entire
valley basically, and just below that -- actually on the ground
level, I think all of those buildings were probably about two or
three stories tall. On the ground level there was a lot of
movement going on --

SME-JSOAC: So, you changed your sensors then from -- you'd
taken them off the squirters? You've got one on the infil sight
and one on the POO (point of origin)?

TELEVISION SENSOR OPERATOR: Yes, sir. It was the TV operator.
As I slaved over there and saw the third RPG, so the AWT hit a
suppressive fire. I immediately called for the IR Sensor
operator to slave to me and once he slaved to me, he put a
sensor directly where I was looking into -- right on this
compound and we have labeled as the POO and immediately we
picked up personnel on top of the roof handing off objects. We
can't identify what the objects were, but they were handing off
objects to the lower levels and they were getting down on those
levels and then there was increased activity, up to like 6 to 8
personnel, and they were running around the compounds. ████████

Reading through these documents left me struggling deeply with four questions, still unanswered today:

1. Are we asking our warriors to fight and sacrifice their lives to a failed ideology/strategy?

2. Is this administration steeped in denial or is it *blatantly* misleading the American people?

3. Were our troops actually compromised on this particular mission? Was it an ambush?

4. Why and how did *everything* go so wrong? What recurring events precipitated such chaos and confusion in the battle space that night?

8

Confrontations

Praise be to the Lord my Rock, who trains
my hands for war, my fingers for battle.

- Psalms 144:1 NIV

The grief over Aaron's death was challenging, yet 2012 was still a hopeful year because I was getting answers about the *Extortion 17* shoot-down through multiple channels: my review of the redacted files and conversations with people in the military, some anonymous. It was also an election year so people were speaking their minds amidst the campaigns. The truth was being sifted from the lies.

During 2012 I was also watching Obama's Presidential campaign in the news. His reelection was in full swing and references to the 2011 take-down of Osama bin Laden brought him rounds of applause. Since the day of the raid, he'd been exploiting the SEALs' victory, while ignoring the fact that he oversaw the largest loss of life in Naval Special Warfare history only three months later. In addition to his "I," "Me," "My" speech on May 1, 2011, he had touted the raid shamelessly and continuously.[1] A year later in 2012, President Obama's supporters had taken the baton and were running with it in the media—removing the threat of OBL was a top reason to reelect BHO.[2]

It was time to set the record straight. The full impact of the actions in the White House and their announcing the involvement of the Navy SEALs in the slaying of Osama bin Laden needed to be known. Karen and I wanted to bring attention to the breach of national security that Vice President Biden committed just days after the Navy SEALs completed Operation Neptune Spear.

We were not alone.

Another organization, OpSecTeam, was also speaking out about national security. Maintaining proper OpSec, or operational security, can determine the success or failure of a mission. So they produced a vital twenty-two minute video on the importance of operational security, hoping it would at least improve the discretion of our government. The video was circulated globally and entitled, "Dishonorable Disclosures: How Leaks and Politics Threaten National Security."[3] It had over 5.4 million views.

Several former military members appeared in the "Dishonorable Disclosures" video asking the president to respect the code of silence needed for our Special Ops missions.

The news media was continuing to leak information related to other al Qaeda stories in May 2012, which led FBI Director Robert Mueller to declare that, "Leaks such as this threaten ongoing operations, puts at risk the lives of sources, makes it much more difficult to recruit sources, and damages our relationships with our foreign partners."[4] So the mission of the people speaking out in the OpSec video released on August 15, 2012, was simple: "Stop the politicians from politically capitalizing on national security operations and secrets." Karen and I understood all too well the threats of operational security leaks.

OpSecTeam, Veterans for a Strong America, and other organizations held a common concern about protecting our national security. Veterans for a Strong America (VSA) voiced their mission as:

> a non-partisan action organization dedicated to educating the public, members of Congress and the Executive Branch about a strong national defense, robust foreign policy and building a military that is second to none. The challenges America faces require bold leadership and a steady commitment – VSA believes that America's veterans will provide the leadership and commitment necessary to keep America safe.[5]

VSA approached Karen and me to voice our mutual concerns about intelligence, operational security, and the leaks coming from The White House in a series of brief advertisements and public service announcements. Karen and I had an opportunity to share Aaron's story with America, and particularly his concerns after the Osama bin Laden raid.

The disclosures coming from the White House had put a target on our son's back as well as the backs of every man and woman either on or working with a SEAL Team. And their families! Regarding Obama's campaign promises, as well as statements by the Obama regime and the media: even one breach of national security by the White House was not the kind of "Change" Karen and I could believe in.

The mystery that once shrouded the power of the Navy SEALs seemed to be exposed. It was as if I were witnessing a modern day betrayal paralleling the biblical story of Samson and Delilah. A Delilah had compromised our nation's great Samson, the Navy SEALs—someone was leaking the secrets of our great warriors. That Delilah was someone in our own government, along with the media, and possibly in the Afghan government as well.

Several of the VSA videos about Aaron's story were being circulated widely, and were integrated as presidential campaign ads for candidate Mitt Romney, exposing the seriousness of what the Obama Administration was doing to our military. These ads led us to be interviewed on Sean Hannity's Fox News program. I had to speak my mind to the nation. Here is an excerpt of the interview:[6]

Billy: Sean, it's all the same. The Benghazi cover-up, what's going on in the Middle East, what's going on in Afghanistan is all because of this president's ideology and the strategy being used by our military and our president is directly responsible for the Rules of Engagement. Let me just say this: on the night that *Extortion 17* was shot down, this is all from the military, we learned that the Afghan National Army, the Afghan National Police, the Afghan Security Ministry are *all* involved in every single Special Ops mission. In the pre-planning, the post-Op, they know the flight routes of the choppers. That chopper flew in there that night in a place that had already been cleared *seven* times, according to our military, by our warriors and turned back over to the Afghans. A three-and-a-half-hour firefight underway, and our chopper flew in with an AC-130 gunship in the air, two AH-64s, and they were not allowed to give any pre-assault fire. They landed the chopper like it was landing at Walmart, even though a firefight was underway. When the chopper was shot down, neither the AC-130 or the two AH-64s allowed to take out the savages who fired the RPGs because they were standing on a tower, and because of the Rules of Engagement, they didn't know if there might be friendlies in the building. These Rules of Engagement are criminal for our warriors.

Sean: I agree with all of that.

Karen: If I could add something to that as well, we also found out in the testimony of one the commanders in the field that he actually said, "something like this was bound to eventually happen."

Sean: That's sad.

Billy: That's exactly right, that's exactly right.

Sean: I saw that. Last question; and I'm running out of time, but do you want Obama to *stop* spiking the football on Bin Laden on the campaign trail?

Billy: Well, he doesn't have the character to quit, because everything is about President Obama, always about, but, yes, we want him to stop spiking the football and we want him to leave as Commander-in-Chief. We want the Rules of Engagement changed and we want some high-up military officer to have the courage and risk all and scream out, 'What is happening to our warriors?' Somebody *please* have the courage to protect our warriors instead of protecting this Commander-in-Chief and his cronies.[6]

On the first Saturday after the presidential elections in 2012, Karen and I visited the National Navy UDT-SEAL Museum in Fort Pierce, Florida, for their Annual Muster. Admiral William McRaven and Lt. Colonel Allen West were guest speakers. Admiral McRaven had led the mission, Operation Neptune Spear, to capture and kill Osama bin Laden.

To our delight, we bumped into some very good friends, spoke briefly with them and then continued to walk behind the bleachers where the crowd listened in hushed respect. When I heard the admiral would be present that day, I hoped for an opportunity to have a brief conversation with him since, at the time of my son's death, he was commander of Joint Special Operations Command (JSOC). This was the second time I would be meeting Admiral McRaven. The first was at Dover Air Force Base in Delaware when we received our son's casket from Afghanistan.

Karen and I walked quietly along the back of the bleachers in the sunlight. It was a classic hot, bright day in Florida. I was standing near the bleachers where the audience sat during his speech. When the admiral finished speaking, I approached him, took off my sunglasses, shook his hand, and said, "My name is Billy Vaughn, you probably don't remember me..."

Admiral McRaven responded cheerfully, "Well, of course, I remember you."

I asked if I could speak with him privately. Hesitant, he paused, and then agreed to meet me behind the bleachers after he finished shaking hands and taking pictures with people in the audience.

Karen decided to walk back over for another visit with our friends, so I stood at the edge of the aluminum bleachers and waited quietly by myself. By the time she returned, the admiral was heading toward me. She stopped short, under the shade of an oak tree nearby, respectfully staying out of the way so I could speak with him privately.

As the admiral approached, I spoke quickly, not wanting to waste any time with pleasantries. "Sir, I just wanted to know if anything is being done differently to protect the lives of our men in battle."

Since Admiral McRaven told me he knew who I was, I thought I didn't have to explain my connection to the *Extortion 17* shoot-down. He had replaced Admiral Olson, as US Special Operations Commander, just a few days after Aaron died, and I wanted to know if the military strategy had changed.

I meant this in the most respectful way, but for some reason he became irritated when he spoke with me, "What's the matter with you? Don't you think I care about every guy we lose?"

I responded respectfully, "Well, Sir, I'm hoping you can share some things that will convince me that you do."

I genuinely hoped that a man in his position would know if anything had changed since *Extortion 17* went down. I felt the burden as a parent to make sure that nothing like this ever happened again to our military. Admiral McRaven got defensive, put his hand on my shoulder and drew me closer to him with a smirk on his face, which was quickly becoming a brighter shade of red, and said, "Let me give you a few facts. *IF* your son did die..."

In lightning speed I raised my tone higher than his and said, "What do you mean '*IF*' my son was killed? You said you recognized me, and you knew who I was. I'm the father of Aaron Vaughn and he *was* killed."

This was not going well. There had not been a single military officer who had shown any notion of disrespect toward me since Aaron had died. He flashed a deer in the headlights look, and then immediately apologized. "I'm sorry, I didn't recognize you."

I can't remember what he said next, but he gave me the impression that he thought my son was connected to Benghazi. "I'm not talking about Benghazi. My son was killed on August 6, 2011." At this point I was thinking, "he's just another politician. He pretended to know who I was, and now he's pretending to know something about me that he really didn't remember."

I went on, "You can smile and smirk if you want to, Sir, but let me give *you* three facts..."

Interrupting me nearly mid-sentence, he raised his voice and said, "Okay, I know who you are!"

Ignoring the interruption and its content, I continued quickly, "Sir, why was there no pre-assault fire that night?"

He snapped back, "They can get pre-assault fire any time they want it!"

I responded, "Well, Sir, according to the sworn testimony, they can almost never get pre-assault fire."[7]

His next words only fueled the fire. "Well, what do *you* want to do, shoot up an entire village?"

"No Sir, but according to the sworn testimony, the village was on the ridges of the valley. There had already been a three-and-a-half hour operation underway and the chopper was shot down *in* the valley. Also, after the chopper was shot down, the Air Weapons Team did not take out the men who shot the RPG because there might have been friendlies in the building below the tower."

In a calmer tone he said, "There were a lot of mistakes made that night. This war is complicated."

This last comment—sort of a confession—struck me. There are mistakes made in every operation; I'm willing to admit that. But I was primarily concerned about the ideology causing our men to die needlessly. It was also the timing of the way Admiral McRaven said, "This war is complicated," because I was just previously forewarned by someone in Washington, D.C. that the flag officers, like Admiral McRaven, are known to say these very words when they want to avoid questioning. It seemed to imply that I could not possibly understand if he were to go into greater detail.

I was now experiencing this warning firsthand.

Unfortunately, I didn't have the chance to tell him the third fact, and he still *never* answered my concern on whether he was doing anything differently to protect our men in the battlefield. So all I could say was, "Sir, a man in your position, if he had the nuts and the guts, could speak up and change the way we conduct this war, and save our warriors."

Admiral McRaven, who is quite a bit taller than me, then jabbed his finger at my face.

I pointed my finger back at his chest, saying, "Let me tell you something, Sir. You can make a scene if you want, but there are people watching us right now, and I don't think either one of us want that."

He agreed and backed off.

I then calmly said, "What we need to do is get together and have a cup of coffee sometime." In agreement, we shook hands, and he told me to contact his office when I had an opportunity to stop by.

We walked our separate ways, and I met Karen under the oak tree. As we headed toward the parking lot, she asked, "What'd he say?"

I told her, "It didn't go so good." We got back in our car and I explained what had happened while we drove north.

I respect the fact that Admiral McRaven appeared to be a man who was willing to stand up for what he believed in, even if I disagreed with him. I would imagine the entire encounter at the Navy SEAL Museum gave him a lot to think about, and neither of us anticipated the reaction we got from each other.

The following week, I received an e-mail from someone on his staff. I was being invited to visit his office. I spoke on the phone with the staff member and explained that it was very close to Thanksgiving, and told them I would call them after the holiday.

I didn't get the chance to call back before they reached out to me again.

Around the first week of December, his Chief of Staff called and said, "Mr. Vaughn, Admiral McRaven would like to pay you and Mrs. Vaughn a visit." The visit was scheduled for January 4, 2013.

9

Confessions and Cover-ups

Therefore judge nothing before the appointed time; wait until the Lord comes. He will bring to light what is hidden in darkness and will expose the motives of the heart. At that time each will receive their praise from God.

- 1 Corinthians 4:5 NIV

The more Karen and I spoke publicly about how our military is being weakened by President Obama's leadership, the more we were approached by men and women who understood this from first-hand experience. Their stories pushed us forward each time we felt like giving up on this monumental battle.

In late 2012, we had an opportunity to speak with a recently retired Army Ranger who was present at the crash site the night our son died. I'll call him Mr. "X" for his safety. The things he told us opened our eyes and legitimized our concerns—it was the kind of truth only someone who'd been there would know.

"We were scared to death every time we had to go out in those choppers [the CH-47s]. Everyone knows they're not safe. They can't avert attack like the MH-47s. We knew our lives were in danger every time we stepped into one." Mr. X then added, "The MH-47 flies in fast, like a roller coaster ride, due to its quick, agile abilities in air. The CH-47Ds fly really slow, with no evasive maneuvers. They're a huge target up there—like a train coming in for landing. They either do a 'runway' type landing or six to eight push-ups before landing, while the MH-47 burns straight in. Every one of us *knew* something like this was bound to happen."

My mind raced back to the words of the officer at DEVGRU, when he spoke to me about the use of conventional choppers, "Just because you do something wrong a thousand times and get away with it, it doesn't make it right." And "what we'll never know is this: if they'd been in the MH-47, would they have been hit at all?"

We learned from multiple sources that the ARSOA (Army Special Operations Aviation) guys were being run ragged trying to cope with as many dangerous missions as possible. There's a heavy weight on a warrior who understands that their Special Ops training as well as their chopper's capabilities *will* save lives that might otherwise be lost.

Mr. X asked, "From what I understand, the shot [RPG] came from in front of the chopper that night, right?"

"Yes, that's what we've been told."

"See, the MH-47 would have been able to dodge it."

His response brought a physical reaction from Karen. Her head fell to her hands and tears began to flow as he continued, "Their maneuverability is just so much greater. Even with the best pilot in the CH-47, those birds just can't do that." I think this was the first time Karen realized just how avoidable our son's death actually was. It was almost more than her heart could stand.

He gave first-hand accounts of how often the helos are shot at and how seldom the MH-47 receives any damage whatsoever.

He added, "One man made the decision to work the conventional choppers with Special Ops. Once the first mission went okay, it became standard procedure. It didn't make any sense."

When we asked about the ramped up number of Special Operations missions per month, Mr. X replied, "Leadership made the decision to go with quantity over quality. For these officers' OERs [Officer Evaluation Reports], it makes them look better if they went on one thousand missions in a three-month period. They just push us out and push us out even to the point where it puts our lives in danger."

I couldn't believe what I was hearing. But I wasn't completely shocked since other Special Operators had shared some of these same sentiments with me previously:

"They won't let us fight. We're just surviving on the defensive all the time."

"I didn't join to be sacrificed. I joined to fight."

He wore the scars of that night on his countenance. He was there. He'd seen the burning chopper. He'd watched as men helplessly waited to pull bodies from its flame-engulfed fuselage.

And now he had more to say—a lot more.

He explained that shortly after Aaron and the others died, he lost a close friend to the "hearts and minds" campaign of our current administration. He then described the most ridiculous Rule of Engagement I'd heard to that point: "If the enemy shoots at you then runs into a building, you can't follow them in shooting. You have to enter and verify that they haven't laid their weapon down before you can engage them. Basically, you have to be shot at a second time before you can return fire. The same rule applies if they run behind a rock after shooting at you. You have to verify that they haven't laid their weapon down before shooting."

His eyes averted us and he looked in another direction, as though he was visualizing the words about to come out of his mouth, "That's how my buddy died."

On and on he went—each story more egregious than the last. "The Afghanis have become angry about our working dogs entering their homes since they see them as unclean animals. Our leaders appeased them by telling us we can no longer send our working dogs into Afghani homes. I don't know how much you know about these dogs, but their work saves a lot of lives. These dogs carry cameras and other equipment which gives us a chance to look around inside before *we* go in. Then we know what's in there and we're a lot safer."

To me, this is all just plain insanity. Some of our bravest and best warriors are getting out of the military because they are not allowed to fight. As I listened, I felt sick to my stomach, but my anger only served to steady my resolve.

On January 4, 2013, Admiral McRaven arrived in a black SUV with tinted windows. The SUV pulled into my driveway, all the way up to the garage, and Admiral McRaven and a staff member got out. The driver then backed into the street and reversed into my driveway to park. I chuckled because it appeared as though they had intended to make a speedy getaway when our visit was over.

Karen and I welcomed Admiral McRaven and his subordinate into our home. We greeted each other and met his advisor, who was exceedingly polite and gracious. Admiral McRaven was a complete gentleman this time, leading me to believe it would be a positive encounter as I had hoped. He apologized for what happened during our previous discussion and not knowing who I was. I accepted his apology and appreciated his concern. The four of us then sat at our dining room table.

Admiral McRaven started out by kindly giving us his condolences and expressed that he wanted to answer any questions we had. He told us he wanted to help us with our "grieving."

The "grieving" angle must be a talking point all officers are keyed in on, since we've heard it time and time again. It's dismissive and insulting. It's as though any question or concern you have is only due to your "grief," not the very real possibility that your question is valid.

The admiral wanted to emphasize that nothing about the meeting would be political. Karen and I were primarily concerned about our men and women in the military and the questions surrounding *Extortion 17*, so naturally we agreed that the meeting was not about politics.

We started with small talk and about a half hour into the conversation Admiral McRaven assured us, "I just want you to know that the military would never hold anything back from the parents."

To which Karen very respectfully responded, "What about Pat Tillman?"

Admiral McRaven lunged forward in his chair, his face instantly reddened, his voice churlish—as though Karen had no right to say such a thing—he nearly shouted, "What About Pat Tillman? It was just a simple case of friendly fire!"

The room fell silent, stunned.

Of course, it was just a "simple case of friendly fire." The *problem* was it took the Tillman family three years to get the truth about the events surrounding Pat's death. Three years of being blatantly lied to by the United States military.

It hadn't been Karen's intention, but clearly she struck a nerve. Much earlier in our search for truth, we had spoken with a man who serves on Admiral McRaven's staff. In that conversation, he explained that the IRF had been sent in because the Rangers were being overrun. I insisted this was not true, due to the very detailed account given to us at the debriefing. Arguing back and forth, he finally said, "Billy, the damn Army will lie." Then shortly thereafter, he made a statement, which bluntly ended that portion of our conversation, "Remember Pat Tillman."

We didn't know what to say next. The admiral did not realize the full impact of the revealing statement he'd just made. I finally spoke softly, "The military *is* holding something back from the parents right now."

Admiral McRaven said, "What do you mean?"

"Well, there are about twelve hundred pages on the CD we were given at Virginia Beach, and page after page is redacted. It might be because you need to redact the files for security reasons, but nonetheless you *are* holding something back."

There was no response from Admiral McRaven or his advisor.

Further into the conversation, the admiral unexpectedly and with no apparent reason began touting the virtues of our current president. After a comment or two, I said, "Well, look, Sir, you are not going to get me to agree with you about President Obama."

Admiral McRaven laughed and said, "Okay, I know."

A short time later, he became more emboldened. "I *know* President Obama and I see him often. I don't just know him as a president; I know him as a man." He pounded his fist on our table. "And he's a good man."

Politely, I touched his arm, "Sir, I'm going to have to ask you not to mention that man's name in my house."

He said, "Okay." Then the admiral—who said none of our discussion should be political—continued weaving the praises of President Obama into our conversation any time he saw an opening.

By the time of this meeting, I had been personally reviewing the redacted files we received at Virginia Beach for almost a year. I was very well up-to-date with the material, but felt I'd receive a fuller picture of the shoot-down through Admiral McRaven's eyes. Would they have the answers to my questions? I didn't know—but I had been hopeful.

That didn't last long.

I went to my drawer and got out Representative Rooney's hand-written letter for Admiral McRaven to read. Explaining its contents, I said, "Someone from the military lied to Representative Rooney. They told him the Air Weapons Team didn't return fire on the men who shot down the chopper because they didn't know where the shots came from."

The response: "Well, they [air support] *didn't* know where the shots came from."

"But they told the parents in the debriefing exactly where the shots came from—it was on top of a building."

Admiral McRaven and his advisor emphasized that, "They [air support] didn't look at the shots till later, when they reviewed the tape feed."

So I brought the Report of Investigation back into the discussion. "The AC-130 crewmembers saw all three shots, and they watched the third shot come out of the tube. One person in the AH-64 said he saw it from his peripheral vision and another person in the AH-64 said he saw exactly where it came from. During the investigation, a MH-47 pilot did some questioning of the chopper crews and asked why the crew didn't retaliate, and the AH-64 pilot blamed the Rules of Engagement. The Air Weapons Support Team testified that because of the Rules of Engagement, the team was afraid to fire since there *might* be friendlies in the building below the tower the shots came from. That's exactly what the families were told in the debriefing as well."

The Air Weapons Teams sat and watched in their choppers as the enemy walked away victoriously. Our men could not engage them, even though they had a clear view to take out the enemy. Once again, the Rules of Engagement were obeyed and great men, with all the right equipment at their disposal, were left helpless.

While everyone remained cordial, this conversation wasn't headed in the right direction.

After a few seconds of silence, I asked, "Why was there was no pre-assault fire before *Extortion 17* went in, you know, just to soften the landing zone?"

With absolutely no hesitation, the admiral replied, "The Operation was already over. By that time, the Rangers were already in the questioning phase of those they'd detained in the earlier raid and nothing else was going on."

Was this all Admiral McRaven had for his defense? If Operation Lefty Grove was "already over" then why was *Extortion 17* sent in at all? Why was the IRF (Immediate Reaction Force) spun up with such hastiness that routes and landing zones were being determined after the chopper was already in the air? And why was the landing zone considered "hot"?

A member of DEVGRU reached out to us at least a year after Aaron's death and explained with conviction, "All of those guys jumping on one chopper that night meant one thing: something serious was going down. Otherwise, they would have gone in on two choppers, landed well outside the hot zone and hiked in, like the Rangers had done on the beginning of the operation."

Later I discovered, from someone who was actually in the advanced operating center the night of the shoot-down, that there were still small arms fire being conducted on the Rangers as *Extortion 17* was flying into their final battle.

But the final blow of contrast came from a JSOC (Joint Special Operations Command) intelligence liaison also in theater that fateful night. He conversed with some of the SEALs shortly before they boarded the chopper. He stated the following, "I had never seen a mission spun up so hastily." He then went on to explain the reason all of them (the SEALs) boarded a single chopper that night..."The HLZ was red hot and they thought a second chopper would never make it in."

The Operation *clearly* was not over.

The misinformation continued and suspicions rose.

Around this point came yet another interjection about President Obama's qualifications and great, fearless leadership; this time it was in reference to Operation Neptune Spear.

The admiral explained to us that the president had nothing to gain by taking out Bin Laden. He then elaborated on the fear factor behind the president's *brave* decision to do so, telling us "There was only a forty percent chance that Osama was going to be at the compound in Abbottabad, Pakistan."

I told Admiral McRaven, "I'm going to have to disagree with you on that one. I don't think the president had any choice but to go after Osama bin Laden."

He quickly replied, "How so?"

"Because the CIA had located him, and if people learned that Osama bin Laden was there, and it leaked that Barack Obama still refused to take him out, it would have devastated him politically."

At some point, the conversation shifted back to the matter at hand. I asked, "Why were our men on the wrong chopper?"

His countenance became a bit haughty and even defiant towards me. "A CH-47D is just as good as the dark horse MH-47." He countered that he had flown in the CH-47s before and he felt just fine.

So I pointed out more specifically, "Well, sir, according to the testimony of the Task Force Commander [Air Missions Commander], his comfort level was very low using the CH-47s."

r_EX48, pages 41 – 45:

> TF(redacted)CDR: I would say, you know, we train in everything always with ARSOA [Army Special Operations Aviation]. So comfort level is low because they don't fly like ARSOA – They don't plan like ARSOA. They don't land like ARSOA. They will either, you know, kind of, do a runway landing. Or if it's a different crew that trains different areas, they will do the pinnacle landing. So we are starting to understand different crews landed differently and needed different set ups for exfils and pick-ups.

> TF(redacted)SEA: It was a popular topic of discussion.

> TF(redacted)CDR: It's tough. I mean, and I gave them guidance to make it work. And they were making it work. But it limited our effectiveness. It made our options and our tactical flexibility [sic].

Our agility was clearly limited by our air platform infil – where we could go. How quickly we could get there. So when I talk about it, I briefed the boss and he knew it that, Hey, we're missing the enemy sometimes because we just can't get there. We can't adapt fast enough.

We will see what we think is the target, then a vehicle follow and move, and we just can't get an LZ [landing zone] approved there. And then instead of – and it usually became my decision whether to infil real late and then, you know, we are going to accelerate our escalation of force. And then we start taking risk there. And often, I wouldn't go in preplanned to have a compressed time-line where we have to compress our escalation of force and, you know, risk something happening or the thing could blow back...

We explained the costs of, you know, and *that's what we're going through right now...*

But the bottom line is their comfort level is low. If we don't train with conventional helos, we learn to plan with conventional helos here. They brief us in on the process. It's very different than any SOF process. It's conventional planning to a SOF mission.

The following enclosure, r_ENCL B, page 7, lays the argument out very clearly—in life and death color:

On 6 June 2011, two CH-47D Chinook helicopters aborted a mission to insert a TF (redacted) Strike Force into Tangi Valley after they were engaged with multiple RPGs from several locations in the valley; the helicopters re-

turned to FOB (redacted) without further incident. Later
that evening an MH-47G (ARSO) Chinook helicopter was
engaged with RPGs from multiple locations while inserting
the same TF (redacted) Strike Force for the same mission;
no damage to the aircraft was reported.

After my meeting with Admiral McRaven, I engaged in a very
private discussion with a Navy SEAL. When I referenced the admiral's
quote above, he actually, said, "We've [Team guys] said to each other
many times, as the shooters pass each other on the second deck, 'One of
these days some of us are going to die flying on those damn choppers.'"

Clearly there's an enormous disconnect between the men whose
lives are on the line and those sipping tea in the White House.

After that the admiral shifted gears. "If you want to blame
somebody for that decision, you can blame me." He went on to discuss
how it was his decision to mix the conventional and Special Ops in the
battle with no prior training together. He also told us that since the shoot-
down, the decision had been made to begin training them together before
deployment.

I didn't react to this statement. Although this revision in strategy
was a step in the right direction, it did nothing to satisfy my mind that this
would never happen again.

Then came the discussion about the seven Afghan commandos
who were swapped out at the last moment. The questions I was left with
that day still linger in my mind:

1. Why was the commander uncomfortable with the Afghani
   commandos originally assigned on Operation Lefty Grove?

2. Why did the commander switch out the men for different Afghanis?

3. Had our men been training with the first or second group, or both?

4. Who was the commander who didn't want the first set of Afghani commandos on the chopper, and who else may have been involved in the commander's decision?

The answers to these questions could have huge implications. And remember, the Afghani Commandos switched out at the last minute were still alive. They might have been intimately involved in the planning of the mission, yet there is no evidence they were ever interviewed or confronted in the investigation.

Sometime after this conversation, I collected the following information from a Special Operator who had recently served in Afghanistan: "We have told our leaders time after time, 'one of these days a suicide bomber is going to crawl on one of these choppers with us.'" We also heard that some of the flight crews had expressed frustration over the Afghanis taking cell phone pictures inside their choppers and occasionally refusing to exit the bird upon mission infil.

At some point the advisor asked if we had received a copy of the Ramp Ceremony video from Afghanistan. "No," Karen quickly answered. "None of the families I've spoken with have received one."

He promised to send a copy right away. He then went on to tell us the rest of our son's team was upset that an Afghani was allowed to speak at the Ramp Ceremony. That comment startled me momentarily, but I made the conscious decision to file it away mentally and explore it later.

The conversation continued moving forward, however, and we never came back to it.

And then came another round of praise for President Obama when I expressed a very painful concern, "It's hard for me to admit this, but I'm afraid my son's death is going to be in vain because the president has decided that we're going to lose the war in Afghanistan.

His response caught me off guard, "Well I can't *guarantee* how Afghanistan is going to turn out, but I *can* tell you that President Obama is getting us out of Afghanistan."

Only two months earlier in our discussion at the Navy SEAL Museum, he'd snapped at me when I'd said the same thing. His response then: "We're winning the war in Afghanistan."

Had something changed in the previous two months or had he only been honest in one of our two conversations? I came back at him with a little frustration, "Yeah, but at what cost?"

His answer blew my mind: "President Obama got us out of Iraq!"

Unable to contain myself I blurted out, "And look at how well that turned out. Now *Iran* is transporting weapons *through* Iraq to Syria and threatening Israel, our greatest ally in the Middle East."

Still to this day, I cannot believe what he said next, "Well, you know George Bush got us into the war in Iraq!"

This statement literally shook me. It was a childish argument and very unbecoming of a man of such high stature.

"All I can say about that, Admiral, is Aaron had great respect for President Bush because he had his soldiers' backs. President Obama does not."

Since he remained silent, I continued, "Sir, I just want you know that I'm going to continue to do what I am doing to try to change the things that I believe are not right."

"Billy, unfortunately, the enemy has a say in the way things turn out."

He'd made that statement several times during our conversation, and I found it to be very sad that this was his greatest defense for what had happened to our warriors.

In stark contrast, General Jerry Boykin, our nation's former JSOC Commander, made the following statement:

> "If they [the men on *Extortion 17*] had been killed on an operation that was less controversial...where they had done everything they could; when the commanders could look them in the eye and say, 'We did everything we could'...I fought a battle like that in Mogadishu and I had no problem looking the families in the eyes and saying, 'We did everything we could to save them.'"[1]

In my humble opinion, the Obama Administration and its military leaders have figured out a way to make a primitive enemy formidable. And that's a national tragedy.

Karen and I tried to talk to Admiral McRaven and his advisor about the ideology behind the war. However, there was no interaction on their part. The admiral's silence seemed to me to be his consent.

We wanted to hear their thoughts on the increasing number of green-on-blue attacks in which the "green" are our supposed "allies" who wear the uniform of Afghani military, police, and security forces, and the "blue" are members of the International Security Assistance Force (ISAF), comprised mostly of American, British, and Australian personnel.

It wasn't until July 30, 2013, when the Department of Defense released its Report on "Progress Toward Security and Stability in

Afghanistan," that we finally learned the truth about a startling and mostly unreported spike in green-on-blue attacks.[2]

Buried almost one-thousand words into that report, we found news of a 120 percent increase in these attacks from 2011 to 2012, rising from 22 to 48 incidents. Additionally, 29 percent (14) of the attacks in 2012 were executed by more than one person. Prior to 2012, only two attacks had been executed by more than one individual.

In short, more and more of our people are being ambushed by the very Afghani counterparts they've been told to trust after letting down their guard in supposed "safe zones" like dining facilities, living quarters, and other "inside the wire" areas.[3]

Yet in our conversation, Admiral McRaven continuously affirmed that he was comfortable with the way our warriors were being forced to operate. This is certainly not the way I, as an American citizen and a father, wanted to protect our republic. Is it now too politically incorrect to question the intentions of Islamists, who are killing our men and women?

Giving one last jab regarding how "good our boys have it," the admiral shared, "When I first became a SEAL in the 1970s, all I had was a rucksack, a rifle, and a pair of flippers. But now these guys get a cage full of equipment."

I couldn't resist pointing out the ominous distinction. In Admiral McRaven's days, he'd been privileged enough to actually work on *clandestine* operations as a SEAL. His comings and goings weren't being announced in public forums. Now our "secret operators" are on calendars, in books and movies, on the cover of *Newsweek* behind their Commander-in-Chief, on Facebook, and being announced by White House officials.

It didn't matter how much equipment they had access to, once the Navy SEALs were exposed as the group who took down Osama bin Laden, their protection through anonymity—the most vital weapon they'd ever had—was gone.

When Aaron was alive and someone asked what he did, he just said, "I'm in the military." Nothing more. But the political leadership was not concerned with their mystique. They didn't respect it, nor did they want to take any responsibility for exposing it.

We ended the visit with Admiral McRaven in a friendly manner. Before he and his advisor walked out our front door, the advisor kindly reminded Karen and me, "I'll get a copy of the Ramp Ceremony for you." And with that we said our goodbyes.

Sadly, the *only* thing we had all agreed on was that Aaron was dead.

Karen and I sat pensively in our home—alone—for days. We didn't speak with anyone and barely spoke to each other. His visit had left us in deep contemplation and deep sorrow. We hoped Admiral McRaven would have resolved the contradictions we'd noticed, but the conflicts had actually expanded. We were now faced with the heavy realization that one of the most powerful men in the Special Forces world had no intention of changing a single method of operation. Instead, he appeared to be a proponent of the failed ideology that had caused the numbers of dead and wounded in Afghanistan to skyrocket throughout the previous four years.

Afghanistan by the numbers:

I compared the number of dead and wounded Americans in Afghanistan under the Bush and Obama administrations. A startling 71 percent of the total deaths in Afghanistan from 2001-2013 took place in the last four years of war. Both administrations have made treacherous mistakes, but in almost half the time (2009-2013), the deaths had more than doubled. On average, the death toll per year has risen by 429 percent on Obama's watch compared to Bush's time in office.[4]

An even more alarming number: 85 percent of our total wounded in action tragedies throughout the Afghanistan campaign took place from 2009-2012. Again, in almost half the time, the wounded in action increased more than five times under Obama's command compared to Bush—a shameful 997 percent average annual increase. No changes have been made to remedy this. The needless death toll continues to rise.

Statistics Located at www.icasualties.org	American Deaths	Americans Wounded in Action
2001 – Dec. 31, 2008 (Seven Years)	630	2,638
2009 – Dec. 31, 2012 (Four Years)	1,544	15,036

Numbers don't lie.

This is the true cost of "winning hearts and minds."

How could I turn away? What kind of man would I be? I felt as though I was finally digging my way to the bottom of the true issues.

10

The Ramp Ceremony
and Reflections

*For I am convinced that neither death nor
life, neither angels nor demons, neither the
present nor the future, nor any powers,
neither height nor depth, nor anything else
in all creation, will be able to separate us
from the love of God that is in
Christ Jesus our Lord.*

- Romans 8:38-39 NIV

But just when I thought my journey to find the truth couldn't escalate any further—it did.

In an email dated, Thursday, February 7, 2013, Karen sent the following message:

Good afternoon sir,

As a matter of follow-up...
Sgt. Maj. [Redacted] had offered to burn a copy of the DVD he was in possession of, taken at Bagram Air Base when

our son's body was placed on the plane headed to Dover. Would you mind checking with him to see if he's made any progress on supplying us with that copy?

Thank you so much,
Karen Vaughn (& Billy)

The following day she received word that a personal copy would be sent right away. In the email was a gracious note explaining the month-long delay since our meeting in January when a copy had been promised.

Finally it arrived. A full eighteen months had passed since its creation and neither of us had the heart to view it. We knew the sight of those flag-draped caskets would reopen wounds that had not even begun to scab over.

It sat ominously on our counter for the next week.

On a quiet morning in mid-February, I was the first to wake up. It was a Saturday, and it happened to be my birthday. As I walked toward the living room, I passed the CD and decided it was time to watch it. Karen woke just as I was about to put it in. She wished me happy birthday, and asked, "Are you sure you want to do this today?" and then helped me launch the opening menu.

The images were difficult, especially with the melancholy background music emphasizing the atmosphere, but we were fine. This was nowhere near as difficult as I had anticipated. The Ramp Ceremony was honorable and very moving, until suddenly, out of nowhere, we heard someone begin chanting a prayer in what we thought to be Arabic while the screen flashed photos of American flag-draped caskets with American soldiers standing at attention beside them. We would *never* have expected a Muslim prayer at a ceremony to honor our dead son and his military brothers. This was a jaw-dropping moment—we were speechless.

Almost simultaneously we said, "We've got to find out what he [the Imam] is saying." Karen had the idea to split the audio from the video and then clip the audio file until all that was left on the newly created MP3 was the Imam's voice. We called Tom Trento, founder of The United West, and asked him to pass it to an interpreter while keeping the source of the file anonymous. We did not want the circumstances surrounding the "prayer" to influence the translation. Our only goal was a clear, concise, honest understanding of what had been said. Eventually, the audio clip reached multiple certified interpreters—none of them aware of its origins. While the translations were nearly identical, there was slight variation in the interpretation or "meaning," which is the portion enclosed in [brackets].

<blockquote>
"Amen. I shelter in Allah from the devil
who has been cast with stones.
In the name of Allah the merciful forgiver,
The companions of the "fire"
[this refers to the sinners and infidels
who are fodder for hellfire]
are not equal with the companions of heaven.
The companions of heaven [Muslims] are the winners.
Had we sent this Koran to a mountain,
you would have seen the mountain
prostrated in fear of Allah
[referencing the God of Moses when
He sent tablets to the mountain].
Such examples are what we present to the people;
</blockquote>

To the people, so that they would think
[repent and convert to Islam].
Blessings are to your god [Allah] the
god of glory of what they describe.
And peace be upon the messengers [prophets]
And thanks be to Allah the lord of both universes
[mankind and Jinn]."

Just before the Imam chanted *his* prayer to *his* god, proclaiming his name (Allah), an American chaplain gave a short prayer. However, he had clearly decided there would be greater diplomacy in his. He did not mention the name "Christ," even though the refusal to do so caused him to cut an entire phrase from the scripture he'd chosen to recite. "For I am convinced that neither death nor life, neither angels nor demons, neither the present nor the future, nor any powers, neither height nor depth, nor anything else in all creation, will be able to separate us from the love of God," leaving out *"that is in Christ Jesus our Lord"* (Romans 8:38-39).

What a tragedy.

Just after the Imam finished his prayer, General Votel took the platform,

> "It is with a heavy heart that I stand before you this evening, but with strong faith and a clear eye as we gather as one to remember our brothers in arms and return them home. The priceless cargo of this aircraft, call sign *Extortion 17*, was just another example of how we are bound together...American and Afghan warriors; answering the call, sharing the risks, fighting side by side. It became much more than that on the 5th of August, and while a tragic

moment, it became a symbol of the bond between warriors that transcends race, culture and religion. We honor all these warriors here today, no translation to the group here today. The unbreakable bond shared by those who have stood side by side in combat is a bond that knows no difference between Pashto, or Dari, or English."

I don't think everyone in the audience agreed with the General.

Now I finally understood what Admiral McRaven's advisor meant when he said that the rest of my son's team were very upset at the Ramp Ceremony when an Afghani was allowed to speak. If this union were so healthy, as General Votel and other leaders would have us believe, why would some in our military take issue? Why was an Imam given the right to proclaim an Islamic prayer over the dead bodies of our warriors?

I want to be very clear here...while the Imam's comments insulted my Christian principles and views, it was *not* the Imam I was upset with.

It was the American government.

Our son's remains should have been protected and honored. His religious values should have been protected and honored. His culture and dignity should have been protected and honored.

Instead, with his body seven thousand miles away from those of us who would have offered that protection, his remains were subjected to a prayer representing the "culture" of those who took his life.

One of two possibilities exist: The leaders responsible for vetting the Imam's prayer either did not do their job or failed to understand the implications of what would be said. Neither is acceptable.

Great, fearless leaders across this nation have aided and supported the mission Karen and I surrendered ourselves to in October 2011. For these men and women, we will be eternally grateful. Following are public speeches and announcements many newly found friends made on behalf of this cause on May 9, 2013. I pray you'll find value and meaning in their comments.

Lt. General Jerry Boykin:

On the 6th of June in 1944 as the sun came up, there were a lot of America's finest coming across those beaches at Normandy. But they were coming across to win a war. They were coming across to kill the Germans and run them back to Berlin. In my view that was the last real war. That [World War II] was the last time America went to war with the concept of total war because ever since then we've done exactly what these courageous families have talked about today, we've allowed politics to become more important than the lives and safety of the men and women on the battle space, and it *has* to stop. But there is something in here, next to the loss of your sons, that bothers me worse than anything else and it is this Imam praying over our fallen comrades. I'm incensed.

There are two people in this room that have been fighting *hard* to get America to understand who the enemy is: that's Allen West and Brigitte Gabriel. They fought hard. And Americans are still ignoring them and the fact that we would have responsible commanders allowing an Imam to come and pray a *standard*, not a special prayer, right, Brigitte? A *standard* Islamic prayer over the bodies of our sons that have given the last full measure in defense of this Constitutional Republic. To have him come and condemn them to hell is an indicator that all of us, Brigitte and Allen, we have failed, and the others around us, we have failed to convince people of who the enemy is. And I want to say this, there is a Constitutional responsibility when you take an oath that you are supposed to *know* the enemy, you are supposed to *know* his doctrine, you are supposed to *know* his tactics, you are supposed to *know* what motivates him, and the fact that we would do this, is an indicator that there has been a deliberate plot in America, in our armed forces *not* to allow the senior officers or anybody else to know who the enemy is or to understand how to fight them because we don't recognize the enemy.

Admiral James "Ace" Lyons, Jr.:

Now it comes as no surprise that political correctness, regretfully, has infected every level of leadership command in our military today. It manifested itself in our Counter-Insurgency strategy with its restricted Rules of Engagement, which unnecessarily put the lives of our military forces at risk. It cost numerous lives, and thousands with horrendous, permanent injuries all in the failed hope of 'winning the hearts and minds' of a tribal society. This makes no sense. Why and who decided to put twenty-five elite [Special Ops] warriors in a single helicopter? That was my first question to myself when I heard about this tragedy. Sending them in, obviously the mission was compromised, as you all know you had to vet our Special Operations' plans basically with all the Afghans that we might as well have turned them over to the Taliban. They knew we were coming. We didn't provide the required suppression fire. That helicopter is made to transport troops and people. It's not made to conduct a Special Operation in a high-threat area. This was pure Dereliction of Duty—somebody needs to be held accountable...

...Let me talk about the ROEs, which are mind-boggling when you go through and you examine what they are. You can't fire on the enemy basically unless he fires at you first. If you see the enemy walking away from an IED that he just planted, you can't fire at him. This is nonsense! This costs thousands of lives and injuries. The same way you cannot fire into an area if civilians are present. The enemy knows our ROEs better than we do. They use it to their advantage.

We know based on the latest Pew Survey of Muslim countries throughout the world, they want Islamic law to be the governing law of their country. They do not want our concept of freedom and democracy. We know that more than eighty percent of the Mosques in this country promote hatred, hatred of Jews and Christians, and promote Jihad. This is conspiratorial. It borders on sedition. They should be closed down, but of course that won't happen under this administration. Under this administration the Muslim Brotherhood has made some of its greatest advances. While the Muslim Brotherhood has penetrated many of our agencies before the Obama Administration, it certainly has been accelerated under this administration. And I am sure that those restricted Rules of Engagement had an input from the Muslim Brotherhood advisors.

We know for example, that fifty-seven Muslim organizations, wrote a letter to the National Security Advisor for the President, Mr. Brennan, complaining about the training materials that we were using to train our military to fight the enemy. That went to Mr. Brennan, who as you know is our current director of CIA and as some of you know is a convert to Islam, which never seems to get discussed. We know that based on that letter, all our training manuals were purged of any reference to Islam, and terrorism, and Jihadists. The enemy was given a free pass. Not only was it purged, our trainers had to be 'reeducated' and some were disciplined as demanded by the group of fifty-seven Muslim countries that signed that letter. Now does this make any sense? This is crazy stuff! You know a commander's first responsibility, which seems to have been forgotten along the way, is the safety of his men. I always felt that was paramount. I could take care that once we assured that, the rest of it would fall in line, the mission would be accomplished; we would achieve our objectives. That seems to be lacking in today's guidance.

One other point I want to make, you know based on the Pew Report the Arab Spring of freedom and democracy makes absolutely no sense. And the same way going back to the Bush Administration, he was going to bring freedom and democracy to the Middle East. They don't want it!

They don't want our concept. The Muslim Brotherhood creed is 'destroy America from within by their own miserable hands.' Their intent is to replace our Constitution [with] Sharia Law [Islamic Law]. We can never let that happen. Change has to be forced on this administration. What I see happening under the Obama Administration is the ascendancy of the Muslim Brotherhood throughout the Middle East. We dumped our traditional allies who were helping us with the global War on Terror, and now support al Qaeda affiliated rebels, militias, with the end result that the Muslim Brotherhood takes control. How does this protect our freedoms and democracy? This is crazy and has to stop. I thank you all for being here.

Lt. General Thomas McInerney:

This nation doesn't go to war and put handcuffs on our people. And we *have* put handcuffs on our people. And Jerry Boykin is absolutely right, 'How many generals are standing up?' We have a complicity that has been on a slide from when Secretary Gates started firing generals because they were not doing what he politically wanted, which was to come forth with the Rules of Engagement and the different things that have got us trapped in this strategy. And of course that's why President Obama kept him. And we now have very senior people going from this tragedy that you're listening to today that I was not familiar with in great detail to where we are in Benghazi—a complicity not to go and rescue our people. And you saw it yesterday, from the very words of the person that was there, Ambassador Stevens to his DCM Hicks were under attack, and yet the next day, the day after, you have a secretary of state and the president saying it was due to a video. Now that is complicity, and how about you now have two Joint Chiefs of Staff who have been complicit in that cover-up, one who did a report, and the former chairman, you now have two CIA directors who are complicit in it, two secretaries of state that are complicit in the cover-up and two secretaries of defense. Never in the history of this republic have we seen this corruption and this complicity and as Admiral Lyons said, "This Dereliction of Duty." This nation deserves more, and I put out the charge to every general and flag officer on active duty today, 'We didn't bring you up to live this way.' This isn't being responsive to civilian leadership if it's complicit to cover-ups. You are violating the Constitution of the United States and we expect more out of you and these families deserve more. They have given their youth to this nation and the nation deserves more. Thank you and God bless you for what you're doing.

Colonel Allen West:

I think a lot of people know what happened in my career in 2003; they know the decisions I made in 2003. And the bottom line, the reason I was in Battalion Command and made that decision is because before we deployed I made a commitment and I made a promise to each and every one of those family members of those soldiers that deployed in my battalion; that I would do everything in my will, everything in my power to make sure that the individuals that left them would come back to them safe and secure. See, I can rest peacefully at night because I *know* that there are no parents from the 2nd Battalion, 20th Field Artillery that can look at me and say that I did not do everything to keep their family members safe.

If we had people that understood what it meant to get off an aircraft in a combat zone, in a raid, I think the decisions you would see happening and the actions would be different.

If we had people that had ever been in an aircraft and hooked up, and jumped out into the darkness, not knowing what would be waiting for them, that they would be making different decisions for our men and women. I can tell you haven't been an artillery officer: you don't send someone out into combat on an aircraft without first pre-paring that landing zone...by first suppressing any type of air defense that had been around. I also had the privilege of sitting in on that classified briefing [with Congressman Thomas Rooney]. That operation had been going on for *three and a half hours*. To launch a Chinook helicopter in-to the night, to go into an operation, a hot zone; that was something that absolutely violates every single principle of employment and tactics for the United States military. Why that was done I have no idea. I have been on many air operations and I can tell you this: even if a Member of Congress is getting on an aircraft and going down to Guan-tanamo Bay, if they change that Member of Congress out they go back down and update the manifest. *Why* were seven individuals changed on the manifest of a combat assault mission and not updated? We need to find out about that. And the Rules of Engagement...

Those of us that have ever been in a firefight know that within two to three seconds, someone starts to lose their life. And for us to tell our men in women in combat that they cannot fire upon people who are firing upon them, that is unconscionable.

But I want to leave you with this simple point, and I want you to all think about it and I hope that the media will take these words and send it out to everyone: in this last election cycle we had a president and a vice president, we had candidate for president and vice president who had never served in the United States military. It was the first time in seventy-seven years that that had happened. Now I guarantee you, if we could once again have men and women who know what it's like to be on the receiving end of an AK-47, a RPG or a PKM, then they would make better decisions and perhaps our nation would not have more mothers and fathers that are sitting here as you are today. God bless you and thank you very much.

Congressman Louis Gohmert:

Well it was bad enough that we put people in harm's way without the helicopter they needed, without the cover they needed...and it is just so outrageous that the best and brightest we have, the best trained were put in such a situation.

Navy SEAL Benjamin Smith:

...You have an administration that is just—they've never done anything as if their life depends on it, like with the politicians, with the media, with a lot of the people, they've never had to struggle for anything. They've never had to get down in that dirt and fight for something.

Captain Larry Bailey, Navy SEAL:

We're dealing, at Special Operation Speaks, we're dealing with even more lies by the administration. This administration might very well be called the "Cover-up Administration" and I would ask you to get the word out about what's happened in the shoot-down of the helicopter and what happened in Benghazi. These two *failures* or what they call in the computer world, these two "fails," are so similar to each other that I think that America needs to stand up...

And I just want to say one thing...my pastor...has a PhD, Doctor of Theology, he's a brilliant guy. He could preach a sermon and he never even looks at notes. He can quote chapter and verse of the Bible like Allen West can quote out of the Koran, and *I have never heard him mention Islam, Mohammed or Koran*, not once. And I keep pinging him, every now and then I'll send him a nice little reminder, "Hey, when are you going to start talking about this?" *Until our theological leaders start realizing that we are dealing with a theological enemy...*we are going to continue to lose. Thank you.

Brigitte Gabriel of ACT for America:

As an immigrant who came to this nation, who escaped tyranny, I want to thank you for building a nation for me, where I can come and be all I can be as an American...I am so sorry that while we can be together with our families, you will be crying for holidays to come missing your sons who gave the ultimate to save our nation and protect our nation. I only pray and hope that we are worthy of the blood that they shed.

Michael Savage of The Savage Nation:

...I was so moved by the deaths of those SEALs, in that helicopter in Afghanistan, that I wrote about it in my book *Trickle Down Tyranny*-pages 164, 166, and the entire introduction in *A Time For War*, ... but I'm going to talk about the issue tonight because there was a meeting today, I should say a hearing, at the National Press Club, of the parents, of the SEALs who went down to their deaths ...

... You heard today on The Savage Nation that they were told not to fire back at the enemy because they want to win the hearts and minds of the terrorists. You heard today that the denial of requests for pre-assault fire may have contributed to the deaths of these men, and the shoot-down of the helicopter. You heard today how Afghan Forces accompanying the Navy SEAL Team VI servicemen on the helicopter were not properly vetted and how *they*, the Afghanis on the helicopter, possibly Mr. Obama, disclosed classified information to the Taliban about the mission resulting in the shoot-down of that helicopter. And today you learn how military brass, having everything brass except what counts between their legs, who prohibited any mention of a Judeo-Christian God, invited a Muslim cleric to the funeral of the fallen Navy SEAL Team VI heroes who *disparaged* in Arabic, at their funerals, the memory of these servicemen by damning them as infidels to Allah. You heard me, didn't you?[1]

Karen and I appreciate the fact that Michael Savage drew attention to *Extortion 17* on his national radio show and in two of his books. I read *A Time For War* cover-to-cover—it was excellent. The Savage Nation has continuously talked about *Extortion 17* while many, if not most, have completely ignored it.

Where are the other truth-tellers? Is the truth not the least our warriors deserve when they pay their last full measure in service to our nation?

Before Benghazi there was *Extortion 17*.

Saturday, August 6, 2011, was the day that changed the lives of my family *forever*. It was the day we learned our son had died in a helo shoot-down in the Tangi River Valley of Afghanistan. The entire content of this book screams one simple fact—his leaders did not have his back.

Aaron Vaughn did not become a member of our military's most elite assault force to "win hearts and minds." He became a Navy SEAL to fight for this republic and defeat the enemy and I'll tell you right now: *any* American flag officer that does not want to defeat the enemy needs to find another job. *Any* man who sits in our White House but does not want to defeat the enemy of this republic needs to step down. And anyone, especially the vice president, who leaks classified information, needs to be held accountable.

The record will show that the Islamists are responsible for the deaths of these thirty Americans, but I submit to you today that the US government and many high-ranking military officials own more credit for the shoot-down of *Extortion 17* than the Taliban.

Political correctness, building the esteem of the Afghans, leveling of the playing field and failure of the Obama Administration to name the enemy, and to accurately identify the savage ideology our warriors are up against, has made an otherwise primitive foe formidable. With the help of many military experts, including our friends in the military law division of the North American Law Center, we have learned more than we ever dreamed we'd need to know about the complexity of this battleground known as Afghanistan. I've dedicated the final two chapters of my story to explaining our newfound knowledge.

11

Rules of Extortion

*Extortion turns a wise person into a fool,
and a bribe corrupts the heart.*

- Ecclesiastes 7:7 NIV

It became clear early on in our search for truth that to fully understand the story of *Extortion 17*, as well as other tragic events on the battlefield over the last several years, we first had to take an in-depth look at the Military Rules of Engagement (ROE) in use on the night our son lost his life. We feel it's imperative that others understand and grasp the severity of conflict our military men and women face on a daily basis.

The ROE are the "legal" restrictions placed on use of force on the battlefield. ROE is usually part of the daily mission briefing, a set of "legal" do's and don'ts that soldiers must abide by as they attempt to carry out a successful mission, regardless of their *impact* on the mission.

Technically, Rules of Engagement are just a guideline; a set of rules, not laws. Still, they are enforced by the UCMJ (Uniform Code of Military Justice), which leads one to believe that these rules are indeed laws, sometimes used to courts-martial, charge, convict, and incarcerate soldiers deemed to have acted in violation of these "rules."

There are three crucial issues that must be grasped in order to understand not just the story of *Extortion 17*, but the landscape in which our military has been fighting for some time. They can be viewed as three separate but intertwined geographies: 1) the physical geography of the battleground and culture; 2) the diplomatic geography and its relationship to the former; 3) the legal mindset, political ideology and standards dictated by the policies of the present administration, which creates the military environment and ROE.

First, the physical geography: both the Iraq and Afghanistan Wars are unlike any major war the United States has fought before, primarily due to the intensity of urban warfare and the nature of this enemy. The enemy, al Qaeda and the Taliban (strong partners connected to the Muslim Brotherhood and other factions of Jihad) choose to hide among peaceful civilians, fighting from behind human shields. These are not battles fought in vast open fields where the opponents face each other in combat. The wars our military fight now are in complex, unpredictable, urban or mountainous settings.

The enemy is not just any enemy looking to conquer land or power. In Afghanistan, the enemy is a network of multi-national terrorists set on a warped world view and ideological mission.

One thing I learned well from Aaron is that any warrior bent on jihad has a different mindset than that of the US solider. A US soldier, like my son, would do everything he or she could to prevent civilians from being killed or wounded. The wars our military now fight are often in populated villages, where the enemy combatants are intentionally placing life and limb of non-combatant men, women, and children at terrible risk.

Second, it is clear that the legal landscape—the need for the State Department to look diplomatic, even after diplomacy has failed—which attempts to cope with these urban warfare challenges, has only increased the risks to our military. As a result, the Rules of Engagement (ROE) of the United States Military must be examined and understood for what they are and what they represent on the battlefield. Most people think that these directives come from within the military...from military strategists and leadership. Such reasoning would be logical, but employing common sense will *not* help us understand ROE.

ROE are, and shall ever be, a philosophical policy weapon used to further the ideology of the controlling political party at any given time. The power is in the politics, *not* the military. The military is expected to submit to the politics of those in power. Those in political power determine what the mission objective is, as well as the policies involved with the country they occupy (e.g. Iraq, Afghanistan, etc.) for whatever reason, even if it is detrimental to and opposed by, the men and women from all US military branches on the ground.

Let's be clear though about the meaning of the word "submit" in the context of military operations. The only ones expected to *submit* and follow policy (ROE) are those actively engaged in the day-to-day combat operations. Those in leadership positions are directly responsible for the formation of ROE at the flag (command) level. The exodus of field grade officers, enlisted, senior enlisted and special operators, combined with the deterioration of combat readiness, compels one to believe that this administrative direction is a losing proposition for national defense and the cohesiveness of all branches of the military. At the same time, this chaos emboldens the enemy, placing our soldiers and civilian nationals in these countries at greater risk. We have witnessed this first-hand over the last four years due to changes in policy, which began in January 2009.

Over the past four-and-a-half years, a disturbing number of commanders have been relieved of duty, retired out, or been fired by the Commander-in-Chief. This includes those connected with CENTCOM

(Central Command), AFRICOM (African Command), fleet commanders and battlefield flag officers, all of whom have had their differences with leadership and or policies, either publicly or privately. Through the Senate confirmation process, controlled by the Commander-in-Chief, they are then replaced by the administration with ideologically-aligned officers. Politics and policy *consume* those who shape and dictate the ROE. It is the ultimate reflection of those in power and once again, it comes at the cost of American lives.

The third and possibly most important challenge is the legal mindset and political condition of the leadership here domestically, that by extension dictates ROE. ROE represent politics on the battlefield, and politics have no place on the battlefield. This cannot and should not be looked at as a failure of those who fight. The soldier's will to fight, to be successful and show that they are part of the best-trained professional military the world has ever seen, is without question.

This needs to be addressed at its core...a total melt-down of leadership and direction for an entire nation.

Through their actions, politicians put those on the battlefield at unreasonable risk and in so doing, empower the enemy. Instead of victory through mission progress, ROE threaten the mission goals first set in place after 9/11. We are not just losing the war for our warriors, we are allowing the loss to be directed and manipulated by political agendas back home at a human cost on the battlefield. Unfortunately, this devastation has visited many military families in our communities across this land.

For the record, Congress has not declared war on anyone since World War II. We would be wise to take note of all of the funding redirected *away* from the military and *into* political payoffs; all the while blaming a supposed budget issue (sequester) on a budget that has not existed for the last five years. Some of that funding has actually been directed to our enemies, critically impacting the war fighters and their families.

We need to take a closer look at what changes have been put in place in the United States and the negative impacts those changes have had on national defense. The government's effort to sanitize war or eliminate the war lexicon from public view is a direct example of the misplaced values of politicians who only *pretend* to lead and look out for the best interest of our deployed military.

In addition, our government, especially the Obama administration, has extended a welcome to those who seek to harm us. Legally or otherwise, through an outright refusal to assimilate into American culture, some of these immigrants bring the worst kinds of change to our land. Understanding these delicate issues will answer many of the questions coming from the men and women on the front lines of the fight, the HEAVY LIFTERS, regarding their assigned missions and the restraints placed upon them on a daily basis. Since soldiers are too busy to watch what goes on at home (as their main focus is today's mission and survival) it is imperative that *we* watch for them.

Adding yet *another* layer of complexity to this type of warfare is the current military strategy known as the Counter-Insurgency Strategy or "COIN." As part of ROE, COIN imposes a whole new burden for our forces in theatre.

Under traditional war strategies, the goal is to neutralize or eliminate the enemy threat and bring our troops home. Under COIN, our troops are expected to make friends with the enemy. Unfortunately, the enemy is familiar with our ROE and the COIN strategy. As a result, the enemy's counter-strategy to COIN is simply to blend in and appear to be just another innocent civilian and, of course, US soldiers do *not* target innocent civilians.

On the night of the *Extortion 17* shoot down, this reality played a significant role in the situation that Aaron and the Special Ops forces faced. Known terrorists on the ground had already engaged our forces, but because they were running in and among potential civilians, or "friendlies," it appears that all our forces were allowed to do was observe them.

According to Lieutenant Colonel Colby Vokey, a retired US Marine Corps Judge Advocate and former head of all JAG West, who earned his law degree while serving in the Marine Corps after watching fellow Marines being railroaded by the UCMJ, often over ROE:

"Under some circumstances, the enemy knows the ROE as well as our men and women in uniform. After a firefight, the Taliban know they should collect all the bullet shell casings and other evidence of their presence. They often leave no trace at all that they were present. This results in our troops desperately looking for any evidence in order to justify their actions and prevent any kind of allegation that they have violated the ROE or fired at innocent civilians. The Taliban have mastered this manipulation of proof over the past few years and are ready for our men (and others in ISAF)."[1]

Aaron mentioned to us many times over his military career, that among troops on the battlefield there is an increasing sense of abandonment and betrayal. They feel, under ROE, like they're being asked to fight blindfolded with both hands tied behind their backs. In fact, because of the legal minefield the ROE create, in some ways the ROE have themselves become an enemy.

Former Congressman LTC Allen West spoke out in regards to *Extortion 17* in May 2013, and made this very ominous statement, "Those of us that have ever been in a firefight know that within two to three seconds, someone starts to lose their life. And for us to tell our men in women in combat that they cannot fire upon people who are firing upon them, that is unconscionable."[2] The bottom line is that ROE give the troops the impression that they are expendable and that their safety is not a priority.

The mindset of the current leadership here in the United States is critically challenging. It is the political environment that influences the legal environment, which in turn directly impacts our men and women in war fighting scenarios through the ROE. Policy decisions have consequences and in the case of *Extortion 17*, the decisions of the new administration had very deadly consequences.

Part of those deadly consequences came about due to knee-jerk military budget cuts.

The effect of budget cuts on the battlefield is critical to understanding what happened to my son. An intellectual timeline linking Executive decisions and battlefield results is worth exploring.

On February 17th 2009, less than a month after taking office, this administration sent a "surge" of 17,000 more service men and women into the Afghanistan theatre.[3] Military Command had, however, requested a 50,000 troop surge in order to assure success. To be clear, a new Commander-in-Chief with no military experience on his resumé received a request for 50,000 additional troops from military command, and chose to give command only 17,000 troops due to his ill-advised cuts to military spending at a time when our troops were in harm's way. The initial surge deployment entered the center of the troubled regions on or around March 27th 2009.

Since these dates, databases show approximately 1,400 US service personnel have given the ultimate sacrifice under hostile conditions.[4] Then on March 29th of 2009, the administration announced it was sending an additional 4,000 service members into Afghanistan.[5] This brought the total for the initial surge to around 21,000 service personnel. But remember...this was still less than half of the number advised by the military in command positions at that time.

With this surge came the new ideology known as COIN (Counter Insurgency Strategy) discussed earlier in this section as part and parcel of the new ROE. The new Commander-in-Chief was already realizing the destruction and disaster of not listening to his military leaders. Relying upon his own political advisers who had no military background, and worrying about public opinion and his anti-war base political party, he had already focused on the end of US involvement in Afghanistan. They had even made public announcements in a NATO summit meeting in Lisbon on November 20, 2010 that an initial transition to full Afghan control would begin in early 2011.[6] They also announced that US Military involvement would end by 2014, but completely overlooked *any* focus on a winning strategy.

At that time, the Commander-in-Chief vowed to be sensitive to the Afghans needs and their leader Karzai, but also said that it would be "unacceptable" to basically leave our service members as sitting ducks, before doing exactly that.[7]

Yet again, as we look at history and events that have come to pass, this is one of the problems created by this administration and their COIN strategists. They neglectfully left our men and women in uniform as targets of opportunity with insurgents who operate under *no* ROE in a country so totally corrupt that the largest percentage of GDP (Gross Domestic Product) revolves around the drug trade.

The current administration has overseen the three deadliest years in Afghanistan. 2010 was the deadliest with approximately 499 service members killed. 418 were KIA in 2011, the second deadliest year and 2009 was the third deadliest, with 317 US military losses.[8] These numbers are widely reported by the US Department of Defense and NATO among others, and are a shameful indictment of an incompetent, possibly even anti-American Command.

Included in these numbers is the largest single-event loss of life in both theatres of Iraq and Afghanistan, the single largest loss of life in the history of Naval Special Operations, and the subject of this book...an operation titled "Lefty Grove," known by most as *Extortion 17.*"

During the months after Aaron's death, the politically correct phrase "winning hearts and minds" surfaced frequently as an excuse for the lack of protection which led to the fatal shoot-down. However, in all the years Aaron served his country I never once heard him say he was being trained to "win hearts and minds." Aaron was trained to protect and defend our nation by defeating the enemy.

The forced joint operations involving the Afghan military and government, including shared mission and objective information, may be responsible for more failures than successes in Afghanistan. This in no way reflects on our brave men and women in uniform who must serve under these highly challenging conditions. This disaster rests solely on the backs of the US administration, military command, the Afghan government, in-theatre leadership, and anti-war sympathizers responsible for the ROE dictates and failed COIN strategy of the current administration.

The Obama administration and those involved in it, whether directly or indirectly, are the reason for the current ROE, which can only be described as suicidal. The taking away of a right to self-defense for our men and women on the battlefield, while offering false constitutional protections to the opposition under ROE is costing unnecessary and unacceptable losses to US military personnel. The current administration has hidden behind ROE for the empowerment of the opposition that has manifested and embedded itself here at home as well.

This government knows there can never be any form of real democracy in the areas of the world we are now engaged. Islam is *not* a democratic religion and this region of the world is controlled by Islamic rule, often of the most extreme forms. The talking points and the facts are entirely inconsistent. These countries have been warring with themselves and others since the beginning of recorded time. The facts throughout global history surrounding a political faith spans as far back as one would care to research. The lack of education, the lack of basic moral conduct, the lack of respect for children and women, hiding behind traditions and beliefs taught for centuries, is insurmountable.

The fact that most Americans have no understanding of this enemy and even accept their transgressions and attacks is horrifying. This is not a bedrock society wherein one can interject democracy, or change the generational way of life that is handed down from one to another in a vacuum void of any outside social influences or education, which would give any rise to growth of a nation or promote a civil society.

We have touched on ROE and the formatting and application of its use. We've learned that it is controlled and dictated by the wishes of the government in power. We have mentioned the loss of dedicated and wise military commanders. We've also addressed the fact that political leaders and advisers, along with military command put in place by the executive branch and confirmed by the Senate, have the power to cull, groom and replace unsupportive officers in key positions, in order to engender the success of their political agenda, no matter the human costs on the battlefield.

I'm not trying to be political but these are life and death issues which must be addressed. This is a breakdown of facts that influence the development of ROE as well as politically motivated mandates, all of which have been shown to increase risks to our troops. Yet the UCMJ enforces these mandates and ROE, and the military leadership must toe the line or face court martial and retribution from the administration in charge.

Policy and influence, lobbying and direct infiltration, for lack of a better word, of this society does control the day. If you can dictate policy, ROE and mandates to less than one percent of the population (as not all service members are combat forces) then you control the pre-determined outcome of not only the missions at hand, but national defense as a whole.

Some would say the best our society has to offer, the real ambassadors of this country, are our men and women in uniform. What have we done to them?

We have lost our way as a society in the constant convoluting of truths. We are in a colossal battle, and our men and women in uniform are leading the way at the tip of the spear. Yet, the very fabric of what brought us here and the reasons why, have all but vanished. We have placed in power a government that has not only embraced threats from this entity, but now demands from society the understanding and acceptance that *we* need to change rather than protect ourselves by taking the fight to that known threat. As stated earlier, from the beginning of this particular administration in 2009, there seemed to be a need to inject a foreign culture into our society without assimilation; ideologies that do not line up with what America has offered to all who have come throughout our entire existence.

When President Obama was newly elected he made a speech in Cairo, Egypt. Since most of the country's leadership did not attend, he spoke primarily to the Egyptian citizens.[9] The front row was filled with Muslim Brotherhood representatives, a well-known terrorist organization that had been outlawed for years in Egypt. In addition, the President's speech made continued references to embracing Islam in America. Shouldn't we ask why?

In 2009, there were "hundreds" of closed-door meetings held by deputies of this administration with jihad-linked groups that were widely covered and identified as being part of the US arm of the theocratic Muslim Brotherhood.[10] At the same time, there were White House meetings on record with CAIR (the Council on Islamic Relations), as confirmed at the time by George Selim, the White House director of the community partnerships. These meetings took place with different departments and agencies, who met on numerous topics with CAIR, along with their lobbyists and others. CAIR as an organization is extremely controversial, known to be directly connected with numerous terrorist organizations, including the Muslim Brotherhood.

Also in 2009, CAIR was named an "unindicted conspirator" in the Holy Land Foundation conspiracy to smuggle funds to Hamas.[11] This group is an identified Jihadi affiliate of the Egypt based Brotherhood. Ask yourself why CAIR remained "unindicted" if these connections were made and people affiliated with them were sentenced and sent to prison? More recently, we have watched as this administration has sent multiple aid packages to the Palestinian Authority. John Kerry put together an estimated $4 billion in aid through the State Department, circumventing Congress.[12] Then the Commander-in-Chief added another $500 million of taxpayer funded aid to the Palestinian Authority, through a one page Executive Order also waiving the restrictions set by Congress, using

"National Security" interests as the reason.[13] At the same time, it is reported that John Kerry was looking to add another $200 million to the Palestinians, for a total of almost $5 billion in US aid going to known insurgent entities connected through the web of terror organizations that our men and women have been fighting for the last twelve years.

Some lawmakers were "opposed" to the aid, but did not stop it. They were opposed both because of alleged sequestration budget cuts as well as known Palestinian ties to terrorist organizations. If Congress as a whole truly wanted to stop this, they could have, but they did not.

We need to take a look at who has been hurt the most by sequestration budget cuts from a budget that hasn't existed in Congress for five years. While billions in aid were poured into Muslim Brotherhood operations all over the Middle East, our men and women in uniform, fighting the different factions of these groups in Iraq and especially now in Afghanistan, have been denied essential resources and military equipment.

Our own government funds those who aim to harm our soldiers while simultaneously defunding our military. With shocking audacity, the government orders our troops to step up efforts on the battlefield with less and less as they make sure the opposition has more and more.

The same people who have funded our enemies and defunded our military have also created and deployed ROE, tying the hands of our military yet holding them accountable if the enemy complains that we are not following ROE. And never fear! Our enemies (literal war enemies) are *always* welcome to complain to the American media outlets, where a sensational story of possible war crimes committed by US military personnel is more than pounced upon. When the media works in concert as a propaganda tool of the administration, every mission is doomed for failure.

Yet these same outlets lend a blind eye to the crimes committed by those in charge, who are true criminals in their documented aiding and abetting, giving comfort, money and weapons to the enemy. These true criminals then set up congressional investigations in which the people involved through party and politics are allowed to investigate themselves.[14] It all looks fine, as long as the media never prints the truth.

John Kerry waived restrictions and sent $250 million to Egypt, during a time when Morsi was still in his office after the election, which means it was direct aid to the Muslim Brotherhood.[15] (The same terrorist organization that is financing, weaponizing and supporting Jihadi organizations around the globe).

Imagine what kind of aircraft could have been at the disposal of Aaron, SEAL Team Six and the rest of the service members on board *Extortion 17* on August 6, 2011, if they had been supplied with the billions we have been sending to the Muslim Brotherhood.

And yes, we are still discussing ROE, the political policy of the current administration and its impact on the battlefield.

What is happening in CONUS (Continental United States) is no mistake of an inept leader, and directly affects the ROE dictates and holds those in uniform accountable to the policy makers that created the ROE. It has nothing to do with social justice, equality or the things that you are led to believe by a divisive administration and a complicit Congress, or the multimedia bombardment of constant crisis coordinated to set the tone and control the message.

The who, why, and what behind these changes has been on the move in broad daylight, and the question remains if we will ever hold them accountable. The Muslim Brotherhood is well entrenched not only across the Middle East but in our own federal, state, and local governments.

It makes sense when you look at facts. Looking at the influence of the Brotherhood and other arms of the same entities operating within our government, you can see and be witness to the different organizations they have been able to absorb and grant influence. They have crept into and have taken hold in the FBI, DHS, the military (Fort Hood and beyond) the State Department, and a host of other government agencies.[16] They've gained this positioning by administrative appointment of agency heads and department Czars and lobbying (bribes) accepted. Some have been vetted and put in place via Senate confirmation, with known pasts and links to the Muslim Brotherhood and others recognized as terrorist affiliated organizations.

Make no mistake, these people and their organizations are meeting; determining US counter-intelligence and counter-terrorism policy, working in unison, as has been documented and reported within the Department of Justice. This explains why the Fort Hood rampage was determined by this administration and the DOJ as "work place violence" rather than calling it what it was; an outright act of terrorism on US soil committed by a person who is a self-proclaimed "Jihadist."[17] All of it could and should have been avoided.

Through the forced changes in this society, this could not be spoken in public, as it would have been against the allowed talking points for the many changes in progress. Our military is dealing with this on a daily bases under suicidal ROE, and still, they attempt to serve honorably.

CAIR has been successful in the forced removal of over 900 pages from almost 400 government training presentations that they deemed "Offensive to Islam," so soldiers no longer even have the training that our military needs to protect you from threats. In 2009, the FBI expunged all references to the words Jihad, Islam and Muslim in counter-terrorism training manuals, because those words are "offensive" to the terrorists.

How can this be, when you are supposedly "at war" with terrorism and the perpetrators themselves continually use these words as reference for their actions? These words were also ordered removed from the "Intelligence Strategy of the US." However, in the 9/11 Commission report released in 2004, "Islam" was mentioned 322 times and "Jihad," 126 times. [18]

More importantly, how could we be foolish enough to trust CAIR with any portion of our national security? The very words they've expunged were used to convict their known associates in the Holy Land Foundation terror-funding trial.

All of these complex issues drive at the heart of current ROE.

On October 19, 2011, an op-ed was published in the *Los Angeles Times*, written by Muslim Public Affairs Council (MPAC) president, Salam al-Marayati, threatening to withhold information and cooperation from the FBI.[19] This has reached utter insanity. But now you can start to see the imaginary city built before you. I hope you can understand some of the questions now coming out of a military that once had an objective and faced a known threat...an enemy who struck US soil in a terror attack unlike any ever seen before. Before them now lies a convoluted description of the enemy, political correctness, untruths and distortions of fact. Our men and women in uniform have become political prisoners in a country (Afghanistan) whose own identity is in question. They have been left as defenseless targets on the battlefield, while this administration continues to support, arm, train and finance the enemy who seeks to do us and our military harm.

At a Georgetown University event Thomas E. Perez, Assistant Attorney General for the Civil Rights division in the DOJ, confirmed proudly this administration's working relationship with the Muslim Brotherhood.[20] In attendance again was the "Islamic Society of North America." This is the same organization (ISNA) which the DOJ had previously named as a co-conspirator, along with CAIR, in the Holy Land Foundation (HAMAS) terror-funding trial. Stunningly, this administration now works with them and funds them directly with billions of dollars given to the Palestinian Authority and the Muslim Brotherhood.

In these new times, the only ones who have direct access to the White House, the President, and the executive branch are donor corporations, international financiers, celebrities, those who have bundled money, and of course factions of the Muslim Brotherhood. Even though they have been deemed unindicted co-conspirators in the Holy Land trial for supporting and financing HAMAS and others, they are now consultant advisors to the U.S. Commander-in-Chief. This is very visible in the current executive branch with direct input from, and in five or six cases, direct appointment of, Islamic brothers to key National Security positions.

This is where partisan policy and politics unite to set forth the tone and demand for suicidal ROE and the complete failure of COIN. It's impossible to determine friend from foe with this administration, but the deadly results tell the tale.

Although our government has not set out to win a declared war since World War II, this administration is the first in US history which has set out to lose, costing an unacceptable loss of military personnel. The American citizens rally to support the Gold Star families and those service members in need, while this administration undermines their efforts and reduces the fighting capacity of those who are on the front lines of defense.

Our enemies do not have the ability to defeat American superiority on the battlefield. But it's not the front-line fighting that is killing American soldiers. The most dangerous kill zone is being opened from the rear, from home, CONUS, and those who lead from far behind in an air conditioned office guarded by Secret Service.

12

Lost Leadership
and Accountability

Many seek an audience with a ruler,
but it is from the Lord that one gets justice.

- Proverbs 29:26 NIV

Regarding the shoot down of *Extortion 17*, General Jerry Boykin described the severe choices that commanders must often make on the battlefield:

"I don't know who made the decisions that day. I wasn't there. I'm not second-guessing them. But I think from my own perspective, what's in my heart is that as much as I would hate to see collateral damage and would absolutely not except fratricide, I would be inclined to take out those targets and deal with the collateral damage later."[1]

When I first heard these words, I heard the words of a true military leader. These are the words that every parent and every American expects to hear from our military leaders. We trust the leadership of our men and women in uniform to those whose priorities are straight, who know the difference between the enemy and the patriot. General Boykin knows the difference between winning wars and senseless sacrifice. I can only imagine what would have happened on August 6, 2011, if a true leader such as General Boykin had been leading the military from Washington, DC. Would my son still be gone?

But it is also the declining political and military environment described in the last chapter that has laid the groundwork for a weakening leadership structure, loss of faith in the commanders, and increased danger in the field for our troops. In fact, the very foundation of the War Articles prior to the signing of the US Constitution, need to be reevaluated by experts and Americans alike (please see the Appendix for additional history on War Articles).

There is a platform and structured outline that has been developed by a group of war fighting entities from different countries. This can be found and read in two documents, which basically outline international rules of engagement. One is the International Rule put together by NATO, which is very difficult to access, but can be found in Manual MC 362-1.[2] The other Manual is called the "San Remo Rules of Engagement Handbook." This one is more readily available to the public and has been translated into eight or nine different languages. Note that it is only a handbook and is not commonly used by all nations. Right now, none of the enemies we find ourselves engaged with follow any Rules, not even the Geneva Conventions. The only place that this particular outline is in print is in the Army's Manual in chapter 5 and it is known as the CJCSI 3121.01B, Standing Rules of Engagement/Standing Rules for the Use of Force for U.S. Forces.

Introduction states as follows:

A. Rules of Engagement (ROE) are the primary tools for regulating the use of force, making them a cornerstone of the Operational Law discipline. The legal factors that provide the foundation for ROE, including customary and conventional law principles regarding the right of self-defense and the laws of war, are varied and complex. However, they do not stand alone; non-legal issues, such as political objectives and military mission limitations, also are essential to the construction and application of ROE. As a result of this multidisciplinary reach, Judge Advocate Generals (JAG's) participate significantly in the preparation, dissemination and training of ROE. Although JAG's play an important role, ROE ultimately are the Commander's rules that must be implemented by the Soldier, Sailor, Airman or Marine who executes the mission.[3]

The first paragraph of the outline instantly convolutes the reader's understanding. ROE "are the primary tools" but there are exceptions. ROE can be conveniently manipulated by "political objectives and military mission limitations...essential to the construction and application of ROE." ROE are legal restrictions enforced by the UCMJ controlling the conduct of our soldiers in the battlefield. But the ROE can be trumped by political mores and philosophies.

Hence, the number of men and women dying in the military often depends on the policies being dictated to the military commanders, and the political pressure being levied by the Commander-in-Chief to hold accountable through the force and function of the JAG Corps, direct representation of the political whims of those in power.

Another problem is "word-smithing." A lot of what you read is used as public propaganda to make the ROE process look less harmful than it is in reality. General Petraeus was masterful when applying this word-smithing technique in Iraq and Afghanistan, especially in the surge in Iraq, employing the COIN strategy.

The craft of word-smithing is intended to sanitize the realities of war that cannot be sanitized. War fighting is a bloody destructive business and there is no way to sanitize that reality.

Words are carefully employed, for instance, when "war" and "conflict" are used in the same writing with a focus set on humanitarian interests. But there is nothing even remotely humane about fighting a war.

But the biggest problem we have with the mountain of regulatory minutia under the COIN strategy is the now infamous phrase "Winning their hearts and minds" as an ROE objective. This was designed for people who have a low awareness level of what our men and women in the military are doing as they are deployed abroad with a stated purpose to win a "conflict" deemed to be at odds with our National Security interests. Keep in mind that those who are running this war do not want to call it a "War on Terror" or even "war" – instead it's labeled by the current Commander-in-Chief as "Overseas Contingency Operations."[4]

Much like the "Surgeon General's Warning" on tobacco products, imagine a warning label on every piece of military equipment which reads:

DEPARTMENT OF DEFENSE WARNING: Fighting under ROE is hazardous to your health. It will restrict your use of weapons, assets, training and technology, which you need to win this war. You hereby are prevented from full use of your war fighting training, arsenal, and tactics in cooperation with the current political agenda, which includes no endgame for victory.

We can begin to understand why our fighting men and women are extremely uncomfortable with the current ROE. Such manipulation of war fighting tactics by those in political power places our warriors on edge and emboldens their enemy. It sets the stage for creating additional casualties and debilitating bodily injuries. ROE adds an unnecessary and unacceptable risk to the already risky business of war, due to the direct injection of attorneys on the battlefield.

ROE creates a critical hesitation on the battlefield, resulting in a reluctance to fight with full force and affect. It also causes the psychology of the fighter to be debilitated, knowing they could be held legally liable for carrying out a mission under ROE enforced by the UCMJ. A full understanding of history and the foundation for battles over ROE within the UCMJ can be found in the book: *Swords and Scales*, by William T. Generous.

The primary goal in any battle or war is to destroy the opposition at minimal risk to our own soldiers as quickly as possible, and then bring our soldiers home.

However, there is a high level of financial interest within the military industrial complex, all while politics drags on at a high cost to those who serve and their families. This should be particularly obvious with soldiers who have committed to multiple deployments, and the accumulation of compound stress. The expense in blood and treasure goes to the military, their families and the American taxpayer. The benefits or spoils of war go to those who don't fight, but reap the rewards of an extended conflict.

Among the first military experts to highlight the scandals in modern warfare was General Smedley Butler in *War Is a Racket*, which was initially a speech and later transformed into a small book where he wrote, "Out of war a few people make huge fortunes."[5] This notion has evolved further than General Butler and other true military leaders like President Eisenhower could have ever imagined.

Many in America cherish our protections in the US Constitution as well as our right to self-defense. Unfortunately, the opposite has taken place with the new ROE. The intent and ideology of the policy-makers now in power is to take away *more* freedoms and basic rights of self-defense from our active duty men and women. Our enemy knows our ROE and how to exploit the vulnerabilities created by it. The DOJ (Department of Justice) has gone out of its way to give terrorist detainees *our* constitutional rights, which they do not deserve or qualify for. Remember, Eric Holder and his law firm worked for terrorist detainees pro-bono prior to his appointment as U.S. Attorney General.

Even with the increased death of our servicemen and women, the current administration still looks to submit to and win the hearts and minds of an enemy without a real face, country, ethics or morality. This is done under the banner of taking "democracy" to a people completely devoted to a way of life and a system of beliefs foreign to any concept of democracy; a people who are totally committed to eliminating anyone who holds differing beliefs. It is akin to "democratizing" a maximum security prison, placing the prisoners in charge.

Following is a public comment widely attributed to Clint Eastwood: "A pen in the hand of this president is far more dangerous than a gun in the hands of 200 million law-abiding citizens."

More American casualties have come from the Commander's pen as a result of ROE than from any other source in the past five years. It could be argued that the media in support of this administration has as much American blood on its hands as does the enemy.

Are there front-line truths that are altered when information is released to the public? Yes. Are there cover-ups? Yes. So what do we really know? Naturally, unless the public has access to clear, raw reporting on the ground from the media or from testimony of the military on the battlefield as it happens, the public will never truly understand our nation's involvement in wars, much less the conditions under which our soldiers are forced to serve.

Journalists who have tried to write the truth have often been brushed aside, or they find that the editors still have the final word. Consumed with self-interest and emboldened by politics, editors control the content and tell a very different story. It's an old trick to insure that the American public only gets the approved talking points that the Executive Branch want the public to have, for sanitation purposes. The big question is—to what extent will the American people allow those in power to suppress the truth and sway public opinion?

During the Bush Administration, the public was treated to a regular body count from the war efforts in both Iraq and Afghanistan. When the 2,000th death was counted in Afghanistan under Obama, the somber occasion was barely acknowledged.

On June 13, [2012] the *CBS Evening News* devoted a story by David Martin to the Afghanistan death count reaching 2,000, as Martin interviewed a mother of a fallen Marine. CBS was alone. I noticed no coverage of the Afghanistan death "milestone" on ABC, NBC, the *PBS NewsHour*—or even on the MSNBC programs found in Nexis, including Rachel "Our Military's In a Perilous Drift" Maddow.

But the networks were all more aggressive when the 2,000 mark arrived in Iraq on October 25, 2005. The Big Three networks devoted 14 morning and evening news stories to the death toll from October 24 through the end of October, and another 24 anchor briefs or mentions. They used the number to spell "disaster for this White House."[6]

President Andrew Jackson once stated: "As long as our government is administered for the good of the people, and is regulated by their will; as long as it secures to us the rights of persons and of property, liberty of conscience, and of the press, it will be worth defending."[7] Sadly the liberty and the conscience of the press seem to be in short order these days.

The Media is an embedded political propaganda tool, using editorial opinion to destroy the war fighting capabilities of the best war fighters in the world. The media has chosen personal political ideologies over an understanding of what a conflict is in the real world, and a respect for the carnage created in the environment of combat itself.

Media manipulation is conducted without shame or regard for the fallen on a daily basis. When the media becomes a weapon of the government, just as ROE have become a weapon of lawyers, we have an uninformed and incapacitated public citizenry.

That environment is fertile for tyranny.

When the media or political elite want to prevent the truth from emerging, they simply ignore it, or manipulate it (e.g. call it hearsay) if it cannot be ignored. Today, news is most often editorial opinion, rather than true reporting of the facts. The people who by contract and code of ethics are expected to report the truth, more often produce pure propaganda. "What is truth?" once asked by Pontius Pilate. "It depends on what the true meaning of IS, is," according to Bill Clinton.

As I previously pointed out, the death toll under Obama's effort to "win hearts and minds" is staggering. The number of deaths in Afghanistan under Obama has more than doubled in half the time Bush was in charge.[8] The number of wounded in Afghanistan under Obama increased more than five-and-a-half times in his first four years in office, but the media has remained silent. Most Americans are strong supporters of the US military, and the press knows this. I have to ponder what their motives could be for such utter betrayal of those who live and die to protect their rights.

Would the American people have reelected President Obama if they had known the incredible rising death toll of Americans overseas under his command?

This disturbing trend happens not only in the press, but also in their "sister" industry, Hollywood. Hollywood gets unprecedented access, even to secret information, when the CIA or the White House wants favorable attention. But where are the star-filled Public Service Announcements (PSAs) and films demanding answers for the American troops when their lives are in danger?

However, what *should* remain silent; rarely does.

Without regard for the lives and safety of the Navy SEALs, for whom privacy and secrecy is essential to their success, the raid on Osama bin Laden received enormous press coverage...continuous press coverage.

President Obama made sure of it.

Shockingly, of all the Navy SEALs who've lost their lives in this twelve-year-old war, more than half of them (thirty-five in total) have died *since* the OBL raid on May 1, 2011.[9]

This Administration has overseen more SEAL casualties than any previous Administration in the history of Naval Special Warfare. Are you asking questions yet? Because the facts are staggering.

History will expose those who "lead" from behind at the expense of all on the front lines. Those who are not in it to win it are destined to lose. Sadly, some of these lethal politicians wear the uniform, but are nothing more than mere servants of the politicians in power over their next career move.

The forsaking of our military by the politically empowered is unconscionable, particularly when the ROE are altered due to a perceived threat to politically motivated policy as guarded by a JAG (judge advocate general).

Shockingly, under the current administration, full Constitutional protections are being gifted to known terrorists and enemy combatants awaiting trial for attacking either our country or our military. Meanwhile, these same constitutional protections are denied our soldiers on a daily basis. Foreign enemy combatants and known terrorists have rights to justice in civilian courts complete with juries, but military courts-martial, wherein soldiers have no constitutional protections, are good enough for our men and women asked to take a front line position in a war that someone else is running.

Ironically, when our military take an oath to uphold the Constitution, they are immediately stripped of their constitutionally-protected right to a fair trial. Our military personnel essentially become slaves of the UCMJ and the JAGs. There is no legal authority over the US military justice system under our constitutional Judicial Branch. As blood runs on the sands of a foreign land, accountability is solely controlled by those holding the political power, making the rules, enforcing those rules and paying no price for their decisions.

It is important to emphasize that as we go through a brief history of ROE (Rules of Engagement), that these policies and guidelines are rooted in many micro-managed sources of opinion that work in concert with the controlling parties in Washington DC. They can change day-to-day and even hour by hour or minute by minute, depending upon how they apply and results on the ground, which either bolsters the administration in command and their military leaders, or condemns them for the deadly results of that policy mandate, blindly followed by the commanders in the field.

At all times, the ultimate commander in the field is the Commander-in-Chief. The buck stops on the Oval Office desk.

ROE have been around since the establishment of our military. However, those rules were once designed by military strategists to protect the integrity of our fighting forces on the battlefield, avoid friendly fire incidents and work in concert with all other strategic planning to secure the stated objectives of a military deployment or mission.

The war environment is possibly the most fluid environment on earth. Opponents, personnel, assets, tactics, strategies, capabilities, technologies and agendas are in a constant state of change. Circumstances on the battlefield are ever changing as well...sometimes by the minute. For instance, in the shoot-down of *Extortion 17*, no pre-assault fire was given as the antiquated chopper made its way to the hot landing zone. However, *after* thirty Americans were shot from the sky, pre-assault fire was freely granted to the troops entering the same area for the purpose of body recovery and wreckage clean-up.

Keeping in mind the ever-changing way wars are fought, there is no such thing as "conventional war fighting" anymore. In Korea and Vietnam, enemy forces began mingling with and using civilian cover by day and assaulting or ambushing the US military by night. No longer did the enemy dress in bright red coats or march in formation in an open field, waiting to be shot. Nor did they hide in bunkers awaiting a conventional beach landing, like at Normandy.

In Korea and Vietnam, enemy forces perfected the art of guerilla warfare, often in urban areas using their own civilians as human shields. But they were still connected to a nation state structure, fighting for specific territory under an identifiable flag.

The people we fight today do not fight for a nation, a territory, under a flag or by conventional means. They have only one rule of engagement, to kill the enemy, us.

In addition to the unavoidable battlefield carnage of politically-charged ROE, our soldiers have another enemy constantly lurking in the shadows. With the media's help and the partisan politics established in these last two conflicts, our men and women are now under the constant threat of the UCMJ prosecution process. This is unacceptable. We cannot continue to allow our troops to be sent on missions that are turned into death traps by JAGs looking over their shoulders and second guessing real-time events and split second decisions. For the warrior in the heat of battle, there is no time for second guessing. Waiting for an okay from someone not present on the battlefield will likely cost lives.

Aaron often talked to me about situations that arose during operations he'd been involved in. There were times I would remain silent about a question circling my mind simply because I never wanted him to second guess himself in a future battle based on something I'd said. I loved him and wanted him to come home. I understood fully that a moment's hesitation could cost him his life. It's clear to me that today's lawyers, leaders, and policy makers don't have those same concerns about our sons and daughters. The enemy and political agenda always take precedent over the blood of our nation's heroes.

We cannot continue to allow good men to pay with their careers or lives just because life-saving decisions violated politically motivated ROE. Our brave sons and daughters, brothers, sisters, husbands and wives should not be living in the crosshairs of the UCMJ. American taxpayers unwittingly fund two war efforts, the war against our known enemies abroad and the war against our warriors, waged by politicians and attorneys back home. It's time we, the taxpayers, start speaking up.

The UCMJ is a "penal" system made to look and sound like a justice system, which military leaders often hide behind as they look to protect their own career and legacy. Military leaders use the UCMJ to escape prosecution in civilian courts when they are accused of war crimes. But they also run to it to prosecute soldiers for alleged war crimes that amount to nothing more than a violation of ROE. In a civilian court, most soldiers would be acquitted by a jury of their peers for split second decisions made on the battlefield, as civilian courts have the burden of proof and the soldier has constitutionally protected rights. But in the UCMJ, the soldier has no such rights and the burden of proof is on the soldier to prove his innocence, as the political frenzy to prosecute supposed war crimes (or ROE violations) flow downhill, often holding the soldier legally accountable for the orders given by others, or providing cover to those truly responsible.

The UCMJ has nearly a one hundred percent conviction rate because they make the ROE and issue the orders, sometime at odds with each other, then investigate, prosecute, convict and incarcerate in a closed circuit system. This is the tool used to inflict fear for those in uniform and set examples for those who watch from a distance, worried by the prospect that defending themselves on the battlefield might bring the same fate.

The UCMJ is completely separate from the Judicial Branch and is controlled by the Commander-in-Chief as a tool for military discipline. The Commander-in-Chief implements his policy through the General Judge Advocate Corps and its oversight authority. The manual of Courts Martial (MCM) is a manual of executive orders from the Commander-in-Chief. In recent years, Congress has abdicated its constitutional oversight authority in this regard, leaving all power solely to the President.

The question to this obvious conflict is: has the UCMJ, otherwise known as the War Articles, ever been reconciled with the Constitution, the alleged supreme law of the land? There is a continuum of history that has brought America to a juncture of contradictions in military justice that deserves *more* attention. I urge you to refer to the appendix of this book for the detailed history relative to this subject.

Most of us know there is something very wrong, but we do not have access to the information necessary to put the whole picture together.

We know that this administration, the executive branch, and state department have supported and weaponized the very people who have been trying to kill our soldiers as well as innocent civilians around the world. We've witnessed the head of the Joint Chiefs relieving a senior officer from the war college due to outside pressure from CAIR, purposely destroying a teacher of truth and history as it pertains to Islam.[10] Our President's half-brother travels the world representing the Muslim Brotherhood's interests.[11] These allegations also imply that billions in American tax dollars are being laundered through waivers and being unlawfully claimed by the State Department through Executive Order, bypassing Congress and subverting federal laws that forbid the aiding and abetting of the enemy.

Using known organizations and individuals that have been identified as terror affiliates as advisers to this administration, the FBI, CIA, NSA, DHS and the Military, all appointed to positions with unfettered access to National Security secrets, leads one to believe that our government has, in fact, been infiltrated by the enemy.

The new ROE are being influenced and enforced by unsavory characters, many who are not even Americans. Is it any wonder why the rates of KIA and wounded in attacks by those we have trained and armed has skyrocketed over 400 percent since 2009?[12] If these accusations are true, then we need not wonder *why* the enemy has been given constitutional protections, while those who protect and defend those very protections in US uniforms are denied the same. We know why.

Iraq, where so much American blood was shed, has turned into a civil secular nightmare with Iran running through air space and borders to supply weapons to Al Qaeda and other FSA (Free Syrian Army) affiliates fighting in Syria, directly representing the Brotherhood and the organization born through the movement. In this brave new world wherein we share technology and information not only with each other, but also with our sworn enemies, the government and press cannot entirely control the public dialogue. The word *does* get out. Eventually, however, you will see the government pass law after law to shut down law-abiding citizens, especially those in uniform, those who pay the biggest price of all, the true one-percenters in America. These are the people throughout our history who have protected and sacrificed all for the other ninety-nine percent.

It is time to stand up and demand answers and hold people accountable in full public view. It is time for people to know the whole truth about *Extortion 17*, the largest loss of life in the history of Naval Special Warfare, and the symptom of a much bigger disease in our military. It is time to clean up the most corrupt law firm in the world, the JAG Corps.

There are thousands of families across this nation that have been directly affected by battlefield losses resulting from ROE, not to mention all those still sitting in Leavenworth for allegedly *violating* ROE. It is time to hold these people accountable and truly give peace to the families of the fallen, and those who have suffered from wounds, both visible and invisible.

In the end, it is not the identified enemy who has the most blood on their hands; the darkest stains rest on the hands of those in command power, here in the United States...those who have betrayed the ones who trusted them with their lives.

So in the Libyan fable it is told
"That once an eagle, stricken with a dart,
said, when he saw the fashion of shaft,
with our own feathers, not by others hands
are we now smitten." - Aeschylus

A Call to Action

President Obama, you need to step up or step down. If you choose to remain in the position of this military's Commander-in-Chief, you must step up and defend our warriors. You must step up and show the same level of outrage on their behalf as you have shown when the religion of Islam is disrespected.

I tell you today we have sheep and wolves in high places, and they are getting our sheepdogs killed. What is wrong with our leaders? Why do they still withhold information? Why do they still withhold the truths about this enemy, putting us, the citizens at risk? We must *change* the hearts and minds of the leaders in Washington and the high-ups in the military *or* we must see that they are removed. When you hide the truth, you become part of the lie.

And just to be clear, Karen and I know that *our* boy would have jumped on board a hang glider that night, if that's all that had been available. This has always been my point: When our nation is entrusted with *this* kind of courage—men who will *sacrifice* their safety and even their lives to defeat the enemy, utilizing *whatever* is available—it is imperative that our nation's leaders make sure they have the *best* that money can buy.

Anything less should be considered criminal.

I clearly have no desire to tear down our fierce and mighty military. I love, honor, and respect *all* who serve. But if a patient has a tumor, you must *remove* that tumor to *save* the patient. I have no power on my own to remove the disease, which plagues our nation's military. But I'll tell you who does...the American citizen. The power of change has *always* been in our hands.

We've just forgotten how to exercise it.

My son had a tattoo on his forearm. It read ΜΟΛΩΝ ΛΑΒΕ.

Two simple words:

With these two words, two concepts were verbalized that have lived for nearly two and a half Millennia. They signify and characterize both the heart of the Warrior, and the indomitable spirit of mankind. From the ancient Greek, they are the reply of the Spartan General-King Leonidas to Xerxes, the Persian Emperor who came with 600,000 of the fiercest fighting troops in the world to conquer and invade little Greece, then the center and birthplace of civilization as we know it.

When Xerxes offered to spare the lives of Leonidas, his 300 personal bodyguards, and a handful of Thebans and others who volunteered to defend their country, if they would lay down their arms, Leonidas shouted these two words back.

ΜΟΛΩΝ ΛΑΒΕ! (mo-lone lah-veh)

They mean, "Come and get them!" They live on today as the most notable quote in military history. And so began the classic example of courage and valor in its dismissal of overwhelming superiority of numbers, wherein the heart and spirit of brave men overcame insuperable odds. Today, there lies a plaque dedicated to these heroes all at the site. It reads:

> "Go tell the Spartans, travelers passing by,
> that here, obedient to their laws we lie."

We have adopted this defiant utterance as a battle cry in our war against oppression because it [speaks] so clearly and simply towards those who would take our arms.
It signifies our determination to not strike the first blow, but also to not stand mute and allow our loved ones, and all that we believe in and stand for, to be trampled by men who would deprive us of our God-given—or natural, if you will—rights to suit their own ends."[1]

This was the spirit of our founders who stood against the mighty British Empire to gain our independence. This is the spirit of our fighting men and women still today as they willingly lay down their lives for the cause of freedom. And this was most certainly the spirit of my son who, right down to the "Don't Tread on Me" flag still present on the back window of his truck, was resolved in his heart that he would *never* lay down his arms to a tyrant, foreign or domestic.

May we, as freedom-loving American citizens, rise up, speak up, and take our place in history as a people who defended their defenders. Let not another drop of wasted blood be shed on our watch.

BETRAYED

Epilogue

Billy Vaughn - A Father's Perspective

"All that is necessary for evil to triumph is for good men to do nothing."
- Author Unknown

I recently came across an Oswald Chambers quote, "When you fear God, you fear nothing else."

This was Aaron.

There is no way you could have kept my son off the chopper that night...one more opportunity to go after the enemy. I strongly suspect the rest of his teammates were the same kind of men. I can also reasonably assume the decision for all of the men to board one chopper was made by the SEALs themselves. Based on the information I've collected to date, I understand that decision. The SEALs did not fail that night. They proved their great valor and are heroes all.

As I've detailed in this book, there *was* a catastrophic failure. But it didn't begin on August 5, 2011 and it had nothing to do with the men of *Extortion 17*. The failure rests squarely on the shoulders of government officials and military politicians. The elusive, terrifying "Green Eyed Ghosts" are being stripped of their mystique by those who command them. It made my heart sick to recently hear a retired member of SEAL Team VI tell me, "Mr. Vaughn, our leaders are watering us down." God help our republic.

My grandson was just short of two years old when his father Aaron died. He is four now. Recently, he asked his mother if God would let his daddy come home for just a few minutes. He said he wouldn't ask God for more than that. Earlier this year, he and I went to a weekend camp where the boys' welcome gift was a headlamp. He immediately looked at me and said, "Pappy, this is just like my daddy's light!" Later that night, as he and I sat silently around a campfire, he looked up at the star-filled sky and asked, "Daddy, can you see my head light?"

My granddaughter was only three weeks old when Aaron left for that final deployment. She will never have her own memories of her daddy. She won't remember lying on his chest minutes before he walked out the door during their last precious moments together. His daughter's memories will not be recalled by her, but will be given to her as gifts by those of us who knew and loved Aaron.

Although Aaron accomplished many great things in his short life, he never lost his true sense of humility. His heart beat to the cadence of Galatians 6:14 (NIV): "May I never boast except in the cross of our Lord Jesus Christ, through which the world has been crucified to me, and I to the world."

On August 6, 2011, those of us left behind experienced unspeakable tragedy. *Aaron,* however, experienced glorious release. It was his day to claim the promise made to him over two thousand years ago by Christ, his Savior. He went "HOME." He had kept the faith. He had finished the race. If he could speak to you today, I know what he'd tell you. "After all is said and done and after you've accomplished all you can here on earth, in the end only *one* thing matters...what you have done with Christ."

I will also tell you with certainty, that no plan of hell or scheme of man can separate Aaron Vaughn from the love of God that is in Jesus Christ our Lord.

Memories may be all we have for now, but I know we'll be with him again someday in heaven. I'll embrace my son, and he will embrace his own family once again. I will grieve the loss of my son the rest of my days, but I am also left to deeply mourn the republic he loved.

When I began this book, I opened it with this scripture:

Then I heard the voice of the Lord saying, "Whom shall I send? And who will go for us?" And I said, "Here am I. Send me!"
Isaiah 6:8 NIV

Aaron did not become a warrior after he became a Navy SEAL. He became a Navy SEAL *because* he was a warrior. He was that one in a million person who had the courage to say, "Here am I. Send me!"

Writing this book has been one of the most painful experiences of my life. But Karen and I know that *our* fight is not over.

On August 6, 2011, the men of *Extortion 17* valiantly laid down their lives on our behalf. Great men and women in uniform all over this world continue to do the same on a daily basis. It's imperative that we, the people who reap the benefit of their sacrifice, stand up and defend our defenders. Go outside tonight and look up at the sky. Show the men of *Extortion 17* that their story has lit a fire in you.

———— ★★★ ————

It is not the critic who counts; not the man who points out how the strong man stumbles, or where the doer of deeds could have done them better. The credit belongs to the man who is actually in the arena, whose face is marred by dust and sweat and blood; who strives valiantly; who errs, who comes short again and again, because there is no effort without error and shortcoming; but who does actually strive to do the deeds; who knows great enthusiasms, the great devotions; who spends himself in a worthy cause; who at the best knows in the end the triumph of high achievement, and who at the worst, if he fails, at least fails while daring greatly, so that his place shall never be with those cold and timid souls who neither know victory nor defeat.[1]

Theodore Roosevelt

This was the spirit of the men of *Extortion 17*.

What will be your answer to those men? As Aaron once shared with me, we have wolves in our government, and they are getting our sheepdogs killed. It is time we all stepped out of our sheepskins and became the sheep dogs. We need to join together and begin a dialogue. We have many questions to ask, and I, for one, am tired of the double talk and deception our nation's leaders are feeding us. We need to do this together.

But for now, my heart longs for that glorious day when I'm reunited with my boy. I can only imagine what he'll say when I arrive...the same thing he said so many times here on earth, "Dad, you've got to see this. This place is awesome."

ACKNOWLEDGEMENTS

There are a number of people to thank for their encouragement, patriotism and unwavering support: Admiral James A. "Ace" Lyons, Jr., US Navy (ret), Lt. General Jerry Boykin, US Army (ret), Captain Larry Bailey, US Navy (ret), and Lt. General Tom McInerney, US Air Force (ret), Bart Bechtel, Bob McCarty (Author of "The Clapper Memo"), those in Pennsylvania, especially "America's County" (Somerset), and Brigitte Gabriel the President and Founder of *ACT! For America*.

A *very* special thank you to Monica Morrill and Cari Blake for your tireless efforts ensuring that this story would be told. Your hard work, support and encouragement is greatly appreciated...more than you know.

Although the *Extortion 17* shoot down hasn't received enough attention from the Press, many in the media world deserve special recognition. A big thank you to Michael Savage and his staff at "The Savage Nation" for giving the story continued attention; Grace Vuoto, Jeff Kuhner, Joe Weasel, Laurie Dhue, Glenn Beck and TheBlaze TV; and the many people at FOX News who have interviewed Karen and I over the past two years, giving us the opportunity to bring this story to the public eye.

Also a special and heartfelt thank you to those of you who have become personal friends along the way: Ken Clark and Jason Worley of

Grassroots Radio Colorado, Benjamin Smith, Connie Hair, Catherine Herridge, Jim Hoft (The Gateway Pundit), Mike Slater (The Mike Slater Show), Breitbart News, the Fort Lauderdale Tea Party, and especially Tom Trento and Mark Campbell of the United West, who have stood beside us from day one, and the entire Trento Vision team—true patriots.

A special gratitude is reserved for those who continue to serve and those SEALs, Rangers, members of the Intelligence community, and other military personnel who have come to us with their personal, private stories regarding the truth behind the strategy of this war. May God wrap you in His mighty right hand and protect you all the days of your life. May you be honored forever in this great land as the heroes you truly are.

To my son-in-law, Adam: Thank you for all the excellent work you put into this project. Your talent amazes me.

To my wife (who is also my best friend) and the rest of my family...we never thought we'd be where we are today, but with God's grace, we *will* make it till that day we're reunited with Aaron. I love you all.

GLOSSARY OF TERMS

AC-130 Spectre Gunship – a large aircraft used to haul and deploy weaponry, also sometimes known as an AC-130A.[1]

AH-64D – Apache Helicopter, Delta Model.[2]

al Qaeda – a group of Muslims, also called Islamists, or Islamic Radicals who are at war with all non-Muslims.

ARSO – Army Special Operations

ARSOA – Army Special Operations Aviation

ARSOAC – Army Special Operations Aviation Command

AWT – Air Weapons Team

Call sign – a combination of letters and numbers to identify military equipment.

CH-47D – Cargo Helicopter, Delta Model is what the American warriors were flying on August 5-6, 2011.[3]

COIN – Counter-Insurgency

FOB – Forward Operating Base

Exfil – Movement of the military and equipment leaving or exiting an operation.

Extortion 17 – The call name for the CH-47D helicopter.

GPF – General Purpose Forces

HVT – High Value Target

Infil – Movement of the military and equipment to an area of operation and then insertion.

IRF – Immediate Reaction Force

ISAF – International Security Assistance Force – A NATO-led force in Afghanistan.[4]

ISR – Intelligence Surveillance Reconnaissance

JOC – Joint Operations Center

JSOC – Joint Special Operations Center

MH-47D, E or G – Medivac Helicopter Delta, Echo or Golf Models is what the Spec Ops crew should have been on during the August 5-6, 2011 operation.[5]

NATO – North Atlantic Treaty Organization – Founded in 1949 through common European, Canadian, and American national security interests. There are currently twenty-nine members.[6]

OCG – Operational Coordination Group – a conglomerate of Afghan National Government offices.

OER – Officer Evaluation Report

QRF – Quick Reactionary Force

SITREPS – Situation Reports

Squirter – Enemy escapee

Taliban target – A high-level terrorist working with the Taliban and/or al Qaeda.

Tangi River Valley – an agricultural area with a river as a source of water for the crops, which is surrounded by villages in Afghanistan.

TF – Task Force

TS – Top Secret

Wardak Province, Afghanistan – a province, county or region in central east Afghanistan.

Appendix
Understanding the ROE

In the Articles of War, Colonel William Winthrop (1831-1899) writes, "It follows that court-martial must pertain to the executive branch; and they are in fact simply instrumentalities of the executive power, provided by congress for the President as Commander-in-Chief, to aid him in properly commanding the army and navy and enforcing discipline therein."

To be very clear, our constitutional justice system is intended to provide "justice," defined by Webster as "the quality of being just; conformity to the principles of righteousness and rectitude in all things"[1]; however, the military penal system is not based upon justice at all but rather "pertaining to punishment," and this relates directly to the ROE. It is a system by which the Commander-in-Chief can punish members of the military for transgressions against the policies of the commander, including ROE, free from any constitutional protections.

As a result, the soldier is caught between a rock and a hard place. He must follow command orders on one hand, yet abide by ROE on the other, which makes successfully carrying out the command mission almost impossible.

In citing Dynes vs. Hoover, Colonel William Winthrop further states, "Congress has the power to provide for the trial and punishment of military and naval officers in the manner then and now practiced by civilized nations and that power to do so is given without any connection between it [the Congress] and the 3rd Article of the Constitution defining the judicial power of the United States; indeed that the two powers are entirely independent of each other..."

"Not belonging to the judicial branch of the Government, it follows that courts-martial must pertain to the executive department; and they are in fact simply instrumentalities of the executive power, provided by Congress for the President as Commander-in-chief, to aid him in properly commanding the army and navy and enforcing discipline therein, and utilized under his orders or those of his authorized military representatives."[2]

For more than 200 years, the US Congress has abandoned its responsibility to reconcile whether or not the very existence of the UCMJ is constitutional by never asking the question or allowing anyone else to bring the matter before the Supreme Court. The UCMJ remains an Oval Office tool, which reflects no kind of law, due process, or justice.

Our armed forces exist for one reason: the common defense of our nation. They are called into action when diplomacy fails, and their sole purpose and function is to inflict damage upon an enemy by force, neutralize the threat, and come home. How does this set of facts reflect upon ROE and the job of every soldier on the battlefield?

Unlike the diplomatic corps, it is not within the nature, training, or mandate of the military to win the hearts and minds of their enemy.

Troops are supposed to be ordered into harm's way once diplomacy has failed.

Once they are so commanded, to hamstring them with diplomacy-based ROE that cause the unnecessary loss of life is an act of treason, a form of aiding and abetting our enemies on the battlefield.

Winthrop cites from a passage on page 47 William Blackstone's *Commentaries on Law, Volume I.* Blackstone quotes Sir Matthew Hale, once English Attorney General during the 17th century:

> "Martial law, which is built upon no settled principles, but is entirely arbitrary in its decisions, is, as Sir Matthew Hale observes, in truth and reality no law, but something indulged rather than allowed as law. The necessity of order and discipline in an army is the only thing which can give it countenance."[3]

A half century ago, the Supreme Court tendered to Winthrop the title, The Blackstone of Military Law, meaning simply that his influence outshone all others. He has been cited more than twenty times by the highest court and well over a thousand times by other federal courts, state courts, and legal texts.

The War Articles have nothing to do with the constitution or the rule of law. The War Articles are a creature of orders and not law, and they are designed for command punishment, not justice. Common law and constitutional law have nothing in common, and military law has no connection to either.

First, on the Military Command Manual (MCM) committees for the UCMJ, there is the Code Committee, run by The United States Court of Appeals for the Armed Forces. The following quote is taken from their webpage, whereby Article 146 of the UCMJ establishes "a committee to meet annually for the purpose of making an annual survey of the operation of the UCMJ (Uniform Code of Military Justice). The Committee is composed of the judges of the US Court of Appeals for the Armed Forces, the Judge Advocate General of the Army, the Judge Advocate General of the Navy, the Judge Advocate General of the Air Force, the Judge Advocate General of the Coast Guard, the Staff Judge Advocate to the Commandant of the Marine Corps, and two members of the public appointed by the Secretary of Defense. The meetings are open to the public and Notice of the meetings is published in the Federal Register and on this Web page. The Annual Reports of the Committee are published in West's Military Justice Reporter."[4]

Secondly, the Joint Services Committee on Military Justice (JCS) deals directly with the (MCM) Manual for Courts Martial and alterations to the Manual over time.

The UCMJ (Uniform Code of Military Justice) comes right out of the Articles of War, also known as the War Articles. This is only a summary on the topic; a book or books could be written on just the history and evolution of ROE and the UCMJ. But what one needs to take from this is the importance of abuses within the system, which can be tracked through the history of our military since its creation under an attorney named John. War Articles were established during the raising of our first navy, borrowed from the British War Articles that were in place at the time, dating back to the 16th century. This was called the "glorious revolution and King James II outing." The first 69 Articles were adopted by the Continental Congress on June 30, 1775. This was established for the conduct governance of our Continental Army. Note that these War Articles were in place prior to the signing of the Constitution. So, the US was bestowed with separate rules for the land army and rules for our navy. Later, the need to make them uniform resulted in what we now call the Uniform Code of Military Justice, born under this name in 1950 and in force since 1951.

During the Revolutionary War, the newly emerging United States of America was led by the Continental Congress and those who settled the colonies. Time was of the essence as war was being declared, and the endowment to military leadership was based on what they knew from the country they had just left. To establish order and discipline within the newly forming militias of a country that was not yet established, the Articles of War were adopted and put in place. However, these two sets of War Articles, one set for the navy and a separate set for the army, were in conflict with each other. Eventually, they had to become a uniformed code for all branches of the military, the UCMJ.

MCM oversight is closed to public view and protected from public scrutiny. As a result, when the media is reporting on stories pertaining to military law, as in courts-martial, the proceedings are drafted for public consumption in terms the reader can understand, as if it is an Article III court. The UCMJ, a creature of Executive Command orders, directly enforces ROE on the battlefield and with holding soldiers accountable under the Penal Code and Articles of the UCMJ.

One must also address the difference between a "direct orders and orders of intent. A direct order is self-explanatory, whereas an order of intent is implied, expecting a specific result without issuing a direct order defining a specific action. Due to ROE, direct orders can often be in conflict with the orders of intent.

The atrocities of punishment are well documented throughout the history of the military and implementation of the War Articles. It is a PENAL code; it exists for punishment, not justice. Justice in this environment has always been a double-edged sword, designed, wielded, and controlled by the same accusers who order troops to battle and issue ROE. The accusers are also the enforcers, through the JAG corps, which represent the Commander-in-Chief.

So how are those who wield that sword held accountable?

Discrepancies in the War Articles and the UCMJ have a long history. So-called scholars and self-proclaimed experts have defended this system since its inception. Most, if not all, who defend it are from within the system itself. Military command in general, abandoned the defense of the Constitution a long time ago, as Winthrop argues: "Military Justice is much more swift and efficient than Articles III jurisdiction, as Constitution protections only get in the way of a speedy and prompt punishment." This is why Article III courts and the Bar do not see the UCMJ as a justice system and do not recognize it as such. This is also why enemy combatants should have no more access to Article III Courts than our own soldiers.

Disputes over the UCMJ system and its constitutionality, or lack thereof, have been part of a long-standing and well-documented legal and political war throughout many years. The questions asked regarding War Articles during the first few sessions of Congress were influenced by John Adams. Adams was enamored by Roman law and the Roman Republic, as well as its iniquities during that period of history, and that interest flowed into the way Adams looked at governance. Adams admired the "Roman Republic." The problem is that our mixing of Roman law, British common law, and a penal system has resulted in multiple governments within the US, never reconciling the legality of the existence of the two governments as established before and in conflict with the Constitution.

The Appendix Was Provided By Researchers at The
North American Law Center
http://northamericanlawcenter.org/

References and Notes

Chapter One

1. Colt, General Jeffrey. *Report of Investigation* (Crash of CH-47D Aircraft, call sign *Extortion 17*, in Wardak Province, Afghanistan on August 6, 2011), United States Central Command, r_EX 54: 19-20.

2. For more information regarding the governmental errors committed prior to September 11, 2001 and during the War on Terror, see *Losing Bin Laden* (2003), *Shadow War* (2004), and *Mastermind* (2011) by Richard Miniter, *Against All Enemies* (2004) by Richard Clarke, and *Storm Warning* (2012) by Robin Brooke-Smith.

Chapter Two

1. Lemon, Don. Interview with Geneva Vaughn. *Grandmother remembers killed Navy SEAL* and *Navy SEAL is Remembered.* CNN, August 6, 2011.

2. Lauer, Matt. Interview with Karen Vaughn, Kimberly Vaughn and Billy Vaughn. *Navy SEAL's widow: 'We were blessed to be together.' Remembering Aaron Vaughn: wife and parents pay tribute to fallen Navy SEAL.* NBC Today News, August 8, 2011.

Chapter Three

1. Obama, Barack (11:35 P.M. EDT), "Osama Bin Laden Dead," *The White House Blog*, May 1, 2011,
http://www.whitehouse.gov/blog/2011/05/02/osama-bin-laden-dead.

2. Harnden, Toby, "Joe Biden opens his mouth about US Navy SEALs," *The Telegraph Blog*, May 4, 2011,
http://blogs.telegraph.co.uk/news/tobyharnden/100086416/joe-biden-opens-his-mouth-about-us-navy-seals/.

3. Biden, Joe and Obama, Barack (3:23 P.M. CDT) "Remarks by the President and the Vice President to the Troops at Fort Campbell, KY," May 6, 2011,
http://www.whitehouse.gov/photos-and-video/video/2011/05/06/president-obama-and-vice-president-biden-visit-troops-fort-campbel#transcript.

4. Paisley Dodds and Lolita C. Baldor. "Al-Qaida vows revenge for Osama bin Laden's death," Associated Press on Foxnews.com, May 6, 2011.
http://www.foxnews.com/world/2011/05/06/al-qaida-confirms-osama-bin-ladens-death/#ixzz2a4W3gHIO.

5. Tapper, Jake, May 12, 2011, comment on Devin Dwyer, "Robert Gates: We Had Agreed We Wouldn't Release Details About The Operation Against OBL But 'That All Fell Apart,'" *The ABC News Blog*, May 12, 2011 (2:41 P.M.),

http://abcnews.go.com/blogs/politics/2011/05/robert-gates-we-had-agreed-we-wouldnt-release-details-about-the-operation-against-obl-but-that-all-f/.

6. Ibid.

7. Gerstein, Josh. "Report: Leon Panetta revealed classified SEAL unit info," *POLITICO*, June 6, 2013 (12:04 A.M. EDT).
http://www.politico.com/story/2013/06/leon-panetta-seal-leak-92263.html.

8. Obama, Barack (11:35 P.M. EDT), "Osama Bin Laden Dead," *The White House Blog*, May 1, 2011,
http://www.whitehouse.gov/blog/2011/05/02/osama-bin-laden-dead.

9. Harnden, Toby, "Joe Biden opens his mouth about US Navy SEALs," *The Telegraph Blog*, May 4, 2011,
http://blogs.telegraph.co.uk/news/tobyharnden/100086416/joe-biden-opens-his-mouth-about-us-navy-seals/.

10. Academy Award® is a registered trademark and service mark of the Academy of Motion Picture Arts and Sciences. All rights reserved.

11. Stone, Andrea. "Obama Officials Gave Hollywood Filmmaker Access To Team That Killed Bin Laden, Records Show," Huffington Post, May 24, 2012,
http://www.huffingtonpost.com/2012/05/23/white-house-kathryn-bigelow-bin-laden_n_1538847.html.

Chapter Four

1. Doocy, Steve. Interview with Billy and Karen Vaughn. Fox News August 11, 2011.

2. Souza, Pete. "August 2011: Photo of the Day," *The White House*, August 9, 2011.
http://www.whitehouse.gov/photos-and-video/photogallery/august-2011-photo-day.

Chapter Five

1. Anonymous. *Death of a Team Guy*. Exact date unknown, pre-2010.

Chapter Seven

1. Doocy Roggio, Bill, August 16, 2012 (3:20 P.M.) "Mullah Omar addresses green-on-blue attacks," *A Blog Of The Long War Journal*, August 16, 2012,
http://www.longwarjournal.org/threat-matrix/archives/2012/08/mullah_omar_addresses_green-on.php.

2. Lee, Matthew. "Hillary Clinton: Haqqani Network Terrorist Label Decision Coming," Associated Press on HuffingtonPost.com, August 31, 2012.
http://www.huffingtonpost.com/2012/09/01/haqqani-network-terrorism-us-afghanistan-pakistan_n_1848660.html.

3. On September 7, 2012, ABC News reported: "Secretary of State Hillary Clinton said today she plans to officially name the Haqqani network, a violent Taliban-affiliated militant group based in Pakistan, as a terrorist organization."

4. "The TF [redacted] commander considered his options, including a strike by AC-130 or the AWT, but was unable to determine whether the group was armed and therefore could not authorize the strike."

Chapter Eight

1. Dwyer, Devin. "Bin Laden Death Bolsters Obama, Highlights 2012 GOP Field's Scant Foreign Policy Experience," *ABC News*, May 5, 2011,

http://abcnews.go.com/Politics/bin-laden-death-insulates-obama-republican-attacks/story?id=13536671.
2. Lynch, Matthew. "Twelve Reasons We Should Reelect President Obama," *Huffington Post*, September 10, 2012.
http://www.huffingtonpost.com/matthew-lynch-edd/twelve-reasons-to-reelect-obama_b_1811690.html.
3. OpSec Team, "Dishonorable Disclosures: How Leaks and Politics Threaten National Security" August 15, 2012,
http://www.youtube.com/watch?feature=player_embedded&v=X-Xfti7qtTo#.
4. Ryan, Jason. "FBI Investigates Media Leaks in Yemen Bomb Plot." *The ABC News Blog*, May 16, 2012,
http://abcnews.go.com/blogs/politics/2012/05/fbi-investigates-media-leaks-in-yemen-bomb-plot/.
5. "Mission" of Veterans for a Strong America, last modified January 13, 2013, http://www.veteransforastrongamerica.org/mission.html.
6. Hannity, Sean. Interview with Karen and Billy Vaughn. "New Ad Hammers Administration for Bin Laden Raid Leaks." *Hannity*, Fox News, posted October 10, 2012,
http://www.youtube.com/watch?feature=player_embedded&v=rSoTnGtRTBo.
7. Colt, General Jeffrey. *Report of Investigation* (Crash of CH-47D Aircraft, call sign *Extortion 17*, in Wardak Province, Afghanistan on August 6, 2011), United States Central Command. Redacted File r_EX53: page 14.

Chapter Nine
1. Dhue, Laurie. Interview with General Jerry Boykin, "Episode Three: Fallen Angel" *For the Record,* TheBlazeTV, aired on June 27, 2013.
2. Department of Defense, *Progress Toward Security and Stability in Afghanistan*, United States of America, July 2013,
http://www.defense.gov/pubs/Section_1230_Report_July_2013.pdf.
3. A special thanks to Bob McCarty, author of *The Clapper Memo*, for raising awareness on the green-on-blue attacks in Afghanistan.
4. "Iraq Coalition Casualty Count," last modified in 2013, www.icasualties.org.

Chapter Ten
1. Savage, Michael. *The Savage Nation*, nationally syndicated radio program. May 9, 2013.

Chapter Eleven
1. Co-author interviews with Lieutenant Colonel Colby Vokey, a retired U.S. Marine Corps Judge Advocate on July 28, 2013 and August 26, 2013.
2. West, Allen. National Press Conference. National Press Club, Washington, D.C., May 9, 2013. Speech.
3. Gearan, Anne. "Obama Sending More Troops To Afghanistan...Official: 17,000 Is Likely Increase," Associated Press on HuffingtonPost.com, February 17, 2009.
http://www.huffingtonpost.com/2009/02/17/obama-sending-more-troops_n_167658.html
4. "Iraq Coalition Casualty Count," last modified in 2013, www.icasualties.org; "CASUALTIES," *CNN,* last modified in 2013,
http://www.cnn.com/SPECIALS/war.casualties/index.html; and "Faces of the Fallen," *The Washington Post,* last modified in 2013,

http://apps.washingtonpost.com/national/fallen/

5. Lothian, Dan and Suzanne Malveaux. "Obama to send 4,000 more troops to Afghanistan, officials say," *CNN*, March 29, 2009,
http://www.cnn.com/2009/POLITICS/03/26/us.afghanistan.troops/

6. Office of the Press Secretary, "Fact sheet: President Obama's Participation in the Nato Summit Meetings in Lisbon," *The White House*, November 20, 2010,
http://www.whitehouse.gov/the-press-office/2010/11/20/fact-sheet-president-obamas-participation-nato-summit-meetings-lisbon.

7. Obama, Barack. "Remarks by the President in Address to the Nation on the Way Forward in Afghanistan and Pakistan," *The White House*, December 1, 2009,
http://www.whitehouse.gov/the-press-office/remarks-president-address-nation-way-forward-afghanistan-and-pakistan.

8. "Iraq Coalition Casualty Count," last modified in 2013, www.icasualties.org.

9. Obama, Barack. "Remarks by the President on a New Beginning," Cairo University in Cairo, Egypt. Office of the Press Secretary, *The White House*, June 4, 2009,
http://www.whitehouse.gov/the_press_office/Remarks-by-the-President-at-Cairo-University-6-04-09.

10. Munro, Neil. "Administration admits to 'hundreds' of meetings with jihad-linked group," *The Daily Caller*, June 8, 2012,
http://dailycaller.com/2012/06/08/administration-admits-to-hundreds-of-meetings-with-jihad-linked-group/.

11. IPT News, "DOJ: CAIR's Unidicted Co-Conspirator Status Legit," March 12, 2010,
http://www.investigativeproject.org/1854/doj-cairs-unindicted-co-conspirator-status-legit.

12. Garrison, Dean. "John Kerry To Prop Up Palestinians With $4 Billion Of US Taxpayer Money," May 29, 2013, *Freedom Outpost*,
 http://freedomoutpost.com/2013/05/john-kerry-to-prop-up-palestinians-with-4-billion-of-us-taxpayer-money/.

13. Boyer, Dave. July 26, 2013, "Obama again waives ban on Palestinian aid," *The Washington Times*,
http://www.washingtontimes.com/blog/inside-politics/2013/jul/26/obama-again-waives-ban-palestinian-aid/

14. Pickering, Thomas. Accountability Review Board, 2012.
http://www.state.gov/documents/organization/202446.pdf; and Issa, Darrell. "Benghazi Attacks: Investigative Update Interim Report on the Accountability Review Board," *Committee on Oversight and Government* Reform. September 16, 2013,
http://oversight.house.gov/wp-content/uploads/2013/09/Report-for-Members-final.pdf.

15. Taylor, Guy. "New U.S. aid package of $250 million for Egypt fuels debate over support," *The Washington Times,* March 4, 2013,
http://www.washingtontimes.com/news/2013/mar/4/new-us-aid-package-egypt-fuels-debate-over-support/?page=all

16. Gertz, Bill. "Blind Eye: Conciliatory FBI policies toward Islamism hampered probe into Boston bombers," *The Washington Free Beacon* in *The Washington Times,*
http://www.washingtontimes.com/news/2013/apr/23/blind-eye-conciliatory-fbi-policies-toward-islamis/?page=all#pagebreak.

17. Mears, Bill. "Fort Hood shooting jury recommends death penalty for Nidal Hasan," *CNN*, August 29, 2013,
http://www.cnn.com/2013/08/28/us/nidal-hasan-sentencing/index.html.

18. Levy, Janet. "Obama or Romney? Think again. They're NOT Running the Show!"

Family Security Matters, June 11, 2012,
http://www.familysecuritymatters.org/publications/detail/obama-or-romney-think-
again-theyre-not-running-the-show.
19. Ahlert, Arnold. "The FBI and the Muslim Brotherhood," *Frontpage Mag*, August 30,
2013, http://frontpagemag.com/2013/arnold-ahlert/the-fbi-and-the-muslim-brotherhood
20. Perez, Thomas. "Speech of Thomas A. Perez, Assistant Attorney General of the Civil
Rights Division at the 49th ISNA Convention," Washington, DC, 2012, posted September 7,
2012.

Chapter Twelve

1. Dhue, Laurie. Interview with General Jerry Boykin, "Episode Three: Fallen Angel" *For
the Record,* TheBlazeTV, aired on June 27, 2013.
2. Mandsager, Dennis (ed.). *Rules of Engagement Handbook.* SanRemo: International
Institute of Humanitarian Law, November 2009.
http://www.usnwc.edu/getattachment/7b0d0f70-bb07-48f2-af0a-7474e92d0bb0/San-
Remo-ROE-Handbook.aspx
3. United States of America. "CJCSI 3121.01B, Standing Rules of Engagement/Standing
Rules for the Use of Force for U.S. Forces" in *Army's Manual.*
https://www.jagcnet.army.mil/DocLibs/TJAGLCSDocLib.nsf/xsp/.ibmmodres/domino/
OpenAttachment/doclibs/tjaglcsdoclib.nsf/8400639488825BD385257549006019A4/Bod
y/Chapter%205%20%20ROE.pdf.
4. Obama, Barack. Barack Obama to John Boehner, Washington, DC, September 28, 2012;
Obama, Barack. Barack Obama to Joe Biden, Washington, DC, September 28, 2012; and
Zients, Jeffrey. Jeffrey Zients to Barack Obama, Washington, DC, September 27, 2012.
http://www.whitehouse.gov/sites/default/files/omb/assets/budget_amendments/oco_de
signation_09282012.pdf.
5. Butler, Smedley. *War Is a Racket.* Page 1.
http://www.ratical.org/ratville/CAH/warisaracket.pdf
6. Graham, Tim. "Unlike the 2,000-Death Count in Iraq, ABC, NBC, PBS, MSNBC Skip
2,000 Marker in Afghanistan." *NewsBusters.* N.p., August 21, 2012.
http://newsbusters.org/blogs/tim-graham/2012/06/21/unlike-2000-death-count-iraq-
abc-nbc-pbs-msnbc-skip-2000-marker-afghanis.
7. Jackson, Andrew. "Andrew Jackson," last modified June 30, 2013, *Wikiquote.*
http://en.wikiquote.org/wiki/Andrew_Jackson
8. "Iraq Coalition Casualty Count," last modified in 2013, www.icasualties.org
9. "Our Fallen Heroes" of the Navy SEAL Foundation,
http://www.navysealfoundation.org/about-the-seals/our-fallen-heroes/
10. Thomas More Law Center, September 19, 2012, "More Pentagon Incompetency: West
Pointer Relieved of Duty for Teaching Truth about Islam," Published by Joe Miller,
http://joemiller.us/2012/09/more-pentagon-incompetency-west-point-instructor-
relieved-of-duty-for-speaking-truth-about-islam/
11. Shoebat, Walid, August 19, 2013, "Egyptian Official ties Obama's Brother to Brotherhood" *Shoebat Foundation Blog,* August 19, 2013 (8:30 P.M. EDT),
http://shoebat.com/2013/08/19/egyptian-official-ties-obamas-brother-to-brotherhood/
12. "Iraq Coalition Casualty Count," last modified in 2013, www.icasualties.org

A Call to Action
1. "ΜΟΛΩΝ ΛΑΒΕ!," http://thefiringline.com/HCI/molon_labe.htm

Epilogue
1. Roosevelt, Theodore. "Citizenship in a Republic," University of Paris, Sorbonne, France, April 23, 1910. Speech.

Appendix – Understanding the ROE
1. N/A. *Random House Webster's Unabridged Dictionary*. New York: Random House Reference, 2006. Print.
2. "Dynes v. Hoover - 61 U.S. 65 (1857)." *Justia US Supreme Court Center*. Justia, n.d. Web. <http://supreme.justia.com/cases/federal/us/61/65/case.html>.
3. Blackstone, William, and Stanley N. Katz. *Commentaries on the Laws of England*. Vol. 1. Chicago [u.a.: Univ. of Chicago Pr, 1979. Print.
4. "UCMJ – United States Code of Military Justice." *UCMJ United States Code of Military Justice. Article 146. RSS*. N.p., n.d.

Glossary of Terms
1. The website to better describe the AC-130 Spectre Gunship:
http://www.nationalmuseum.af.mil/factsheets/factsheet.asp?id=412
http://www.military.com/video/aircraft/gunships/the-ac-130-gunship-in-action/1956129559001/.
2. The website to better describe the AH-64D – Apache Helicopter, Delta Model:
http://www.boeing.com/boeing/rotorcraft/military/ah64d/.
3. The website to better describe the CH-47D – Cargo Helicopter, Delta Model:
http://www.boeing.com/boeing/rotorcraft/military/ch47d/.
4. "NATO and Afghanistan," last modified June 13, 2013,
http://www.nato.int/cps/en/natolive/69772.htm.
5. The website to better describe the MH-47D, E or G Medivac Helicopter Delta, Echo or Golf Models: http://www.boeing.com/boeing/rotorcraft/military/mh47e/index.page.
6. "NATO Member Countries," last modified 2013,
http://www.nato.int/nato-welcome/index.html#members.